Ch'i Pai Shih

By T. C. Lai

UNIVERSITY OF WASHINGTON PRESS

Seattle and London

Also by T.C. Lai

Romance of the Western Chamber
More Chinese Sayings
Things Chinese
T'ang Yin
A Scholar in Imperial China
Chinese Couplets
Selected Chinese Sayings
Love Poetry from the Chinese
Chinese Proverbs
The Eight Immortals
Chinese Poetry

Printed by Wing Tai Cheung Printing Co., Ltd. Hong Kong.

CONTENTS

Acknowledgments   VI

List of Illustrations   VII

Introductory Note   IX

Autobiography of Ch'i Pai Shih   1

The Paintings of Ch'i Pai Shih   113

More Poems   121

Memories of Ch'i Pai Shih   151

Anecdotes   161

More Seals   173

Appendix   189

Glossary   199

ACKNOWLEDGMENTS

Grateful thanks to:

Mr. C. T. Tsiang and Mr. Charles Wong for reading through the M/S and for valuable comments

Mr. George Kao for suggesting various improvements

Professor Chu-tsing Li for advice and encouragement.

Dr. May-ching Kao Yeung for contributing the chapter *The Paintings of Ch'i Pai Shih: An Appreciation*

Mr. P.J. Hsu, Mr. Chang Tung and Mr. Chang Li-chi for their contributions towards the chapter Memories of Ch'i Pai Shih

Mr. P.J. Hsu, Mr. S.P. Chang, Mr. Pi-han Chang and Mr. M.K. Kwok for permission to reproduce paintings in their collection

Mr. Stephen Soong and Mr. William Hung for encouragement and help in various ways

Mrs. Eilleen Hannah for valuable comments on the translated Poems

Prof. Mou Jun-sun, Mr. Chuang Shen, Mr. Hsu Ping Lin and Mr. Wucius Wong for their interest and assistance

Mr. J. T. Gatbonton, Mr. Rene Q. Bas, Miss Donna Roginski for their goodwill and substantial assistance

Miss Susan Lam for compiling the Glossary and for secretarial assistance rendered

Staff of the Fung Ping Shan Library and the Chinese University Library for various courtesies

LIST OF ILLUSTRATIONS

Frontispiece: Portrait of Chi Pai Shih
Colour Plates:

	Page
Cherries in Bowl	opp. 60
Landscape	after 61
"Dedicated to Foreign Friends"	opp. 61
Children at Play	opp. 76
Drunken Prime Minister	after 76
Squirrels and Cherries	opp. 77
Child Leading Buffalo	opp. 100
Sparrow and Plum Blossom	opp. 101
Maid-servant	opp. 116
Evening	opp. 117
Crane	after 92
Lychees	opp. 92
Peaches and flowers	after 92
Trees & Cottages	opp. 93

Black & White Plates:

Portrait of Ch'i Pai Shih	X
Fish	22
Cartoons	48 - 9
Remembering Pa Ta Shan Jen	54
Cottages & Trees	59
White Lettuce	60
Landscape	62
A Mynah	64
A Duck	66
A Lohan	66
Snow Scene	67
Crabs	69
A Bird	74
A rake	75
Crows	77
An Immortal	78
Cormorants	80 - 1
Landscape	82
Shih Tao at work	83

Chung Kuei   84
Landscape   86
Buffalo & Willow-leaves   87
Shrimps   88
Fruit and Wasp   89
Frogs   90
Monk with Frog   91
Dragonflies   92
Scale of Fees   95
Shrimps   96
Shrimps   98
A Meal at Night   100
Fish and Loofah Gourd   101
Bird in cage   102
Oil Lamp with Cicada   103
Monkey carrying Peach   104
Grapes and Vine   106
Portrait of Ch'i Pai Shih   109
Gourds   110
Crabs   120
Calligraphy on Fan   121
A Preface by Ch'i Pai Shih   122
Boy Going to School   128 - 9
Brushes, Inkstone etc.   130
Lotus and Dragonfly   137
Lamp and Mouse   143
Three Types of Overplus   148
Three Types of Overplus   149
Portrait of Ch'i Pai Shih   152
There is Nothing Like Drinking   160
Sound of Frogs   163
Abacus   165
Crabs   169
Homing Birds   172
Squirrels   174

INTRODUCTORY NOTE

The bulk of this volume consists in the auto-biographical reminiscences of Ch'i Pai Shih. I thought it best to let the subject tell the story in his own inimitable way, which results in an altogether sincere and touching document. I felt my job should be to round it out with whatever materials I can lay hands on, apart from what is listed in the Sources.

I am fortunate enough to have acquired some firsthand accounts in the form of recollections related to me by friends in Hong Kong, especially events that happened after 1947 where the main narrative ends. Many of the paintings reproduced here have not hitherto been published. The seals selected for this volume not only provide aesthetic enjoyment but do themselves tell a story and are revelatory of the artist's thought and personality.

The value of this book is also enhanced by the inclusion of a chapter on Ch'i Pai Shih's art, written by a specialist in the contemporary field.

T.C.L

The Seal: "The white Cottage of Star Pond does not produce ranking officials."

THE AUTOBIOGRAPHY OF CH'I PAI SHIH

When Ch'i Pai Shih was seventy-one, he asked Chin Sung Shen to write his biography and kept Chin supplied with details of his life through Chang Tz'u Chi one of his pupils to whom he had verbally communicated this account. So far only that part of the narrative ending in 1947 has been published.

The present translation is based on this account, but considerably abridged. Names in Chinese are given in the Glossary at the end of this book.

The Seal: "I am a native of Hsiang T'an, Changsha, China."

Chapter 1   Childhood

I was born in the year Kuei Hai, the "year of the pig", 1863. My grandfather and grandmother were still alive. We were extremely poor. Our house was small, rather out of repair, with a drying yard in front. Our worldly possession was just one *mou* of paddy field producing five or six stones of grain a year, but this was not enough to keep five people alive. My grandfather and my father both had to do odd jobs to eke out a living. Odd-job people in those days had their meals at their masters' homes and were paid twenty coins per day. Although this was a small sum, it was not easy to come by because one did not get such work every day. Many people wanted odd-jobs and employers were usually mean and difficult to get along with. Thus, these people had to make do with "fishing one day, drying the nets the next three," meaning working one day only to stay idle the next three. When there was nothing to do, my grandfather and my father would gather firewood up the hills and sell it. That was how we carried on.

The Seal: "One of the commonfolk."

1

My native village was Hsiang T'an, Hunan. According to my grandfather, our ancestors moved to Hsiang T'an from Tang Shan, Kiangsu, in the Ming Dynasty during the reign of Yung Lo. How we got settled in Hsiang T'an I could not tell, but during the reign of Chien Lung, my great-great-grandfather moved to Hsing Tou T'ang or Star Pond in Hsing Tzu Wu (Apricot Valley) where I was born. It was so called because a meteorite fell in the pond in the remote past. It was a scenic spot. Ten miles from there lay the township of Yen Tun Ling. Our ancestral shrine was there where every year the Ch'i clansmen gathered to worship. I cannot remember all the things my grandfather told me about my great-great-grandfather except that they were all buried in Star Pond. My great-grandfather was the third son in the family and he was called San Yeh, "Master Number Three." My ancestors were all farmers and, in those days, farmers were poor people and they usually remained poor all their lives. My grandfather, being the tenth son in the family, was called Shih Yeh "Master Number Ten." He was a straightforward man and whenever he saw injustice, he would speak out in indignation, so everybody called him "the blunt one." He went through the ups and downs of the Taiping Heavenly Kingdom period and during his old age he witnessed the plundering of the palaces of the leaders of the Taiping Rebellion by the Hsiang army. He saw them getting rich, buying land and houses and behaving as if they were masters of the land. He saw how they became government officials, how they took advantage of their positions and how they usurped justice in their dealings with the common people.

My grandfather being poor had nothing to offer these people; and although he never suffered from their oppression, he never had a good word to say about them. My father was the only son and because I was the eldest grandson, the love that my grandparents bore me was particularly touching. When I thought about it, I always feel like having a good cry over their graves.

My father was of quite a different temperament from my grandfather. He was timid, honest and not very effectual. He was used to taking insult without protest, always "swallowing tears" as it were. My mother was quite different—strong and capable and would staunchly defend her principles. She was nevertheless polite, frugal and affable. She enjoyed the reputation of being an amiable person. If my father had not the assistance of my mother, it would have been quite unthinkable.

Speaking of my mother, it is a long story. Her maiden name was Chou. Her family lived very near Star Pond. Her father Chou Ya Jo was a local tutor. She married my father when she was seventeen. On her wedding day, my grandmother, as was the custom, looked over her dowry-box. My mother was a little embarrassed because, being poor, there was very little of value in the box. My grandmother said, being herself from a poor family, "A good girl does not depend on her dowry; a family gets prosperous on its own strength." My mother was deeply touched, and so, only three days after her wedding, she started working in the kitchen and attended to all household affairs. She was always very courteous to her parents-in-law and whenever she had some good food, she always gave it to them first before having her own share. In our village we used to dry hay for fuel. Very often the hay contained some bits of grain and my mother would use a rod to beat it. In a year, she would collect something like five pecks which she would use to exchange for cotton. We grew some jute near the grounds of our house and my mother would occupy herself with weaving cotton in Spring and jute in Summer. Thus, ever since my mother's advent, everyone began to wear clothing made of material woven by her, and my grand-parents were always given the first choice and my father second, and then herself. Within two years the family had a trunkful of clothing. My grand-parents never had so much worldly possession and they were very happy. They used to say, "Our daughter-in-law has a pair of marvellous hands." My mother also reared a good number of ducks and chickens as well as pigs, which all contributed to the family's subsistence. Although all these meant a great deal of patience and hardship, we were in essence a happy family.

The year I was born my grandfather was fifty-six years old, my grandmother fifty-one, my father twenty-five and my mother nineteen. I was quite a weakling and fell ill rather frequently. The doctor used to order that I should refrain from eating this and that, including meat, fish and greasy things. That was when I was still a suckling baby. Because of what the doctor said, my mother went on diet, avoiding all the things that I was not supposed to touch for fear that they might affect the quality of her milk. Of course, poor people did not have much meat or fish anyway, but on festivals, we would have a little of each, but my mother would scrupulously stay away from them. That was the way she tried to preserve my health. When I come to think of it, I often feel that I owe her a great deal and regret that I was not able to spend more time with her when I grew up.

I was given the name "Shun Chih" and my grandparents all called me "Ah Chih." When I became a carpenter, my employers all called me "Carpenter Chih." The more courteous ones called me "Master Carpenter Chih." My fancy name was "Wei Ch'ing," but my grandfather gave me another-"Lan Ting." The name "Huang" by which I was generally known was given by my tutor, who also called me "Pin Sheng." Not far from my home was a mail-station called "Pai Shih P'u" (White Stone Market) and so my tutor gave me another appellation "White Stone Hermit," but people would just call me "Pai Shih." So I always called myself "Ch'i Pai Shih." I had other names like "Wood Devotee," "Wood-man," and so on, all of which testified to my having been a carpenter, a fact which was not to be forgotten. I had yet other names like "The Old Citizen of Apricot Valley," "The Descendant of the Old House at Star Pond," "The Old Farmer of Hsiang," which are used to commemorate the locale where I was born. "Ch'i Ta" is a play on the proverb "Ch'i ta fei ou" which also aptly signified my state of being the first born. "Chi Yuan", "Chi P'ing," "Lao P'ing," "P'ing Weng," "Chi P'ing T'ang Chu Jen," "Chi Huan Hsien Nu"—all these to signify my state of being constantly on the move like duckweed (p'ing) in the wind. Also the character "P'ing" is

5

homophonous with the word "Pin." (瀕) The names "Chieh Shan Yin Kuan Chu Che," "Chieh Shan Weng" (Borrowed Hill Old Man) were used to remind me that I should be contented wherever I happened to be. "A Richman with Three Hundred Stone Seals" is an ironic way of saying that I possessed three hundred stone seals. All these *nom de plumes* have been used on my paintings or seals. After I attained middle age, people including foreigners, knew me only as "Ch'i Huang," or "Pai Shih," to the neglect of all the others. None knew the name "Ch'i Shun Chih" except my village elders.

The Seal: "Born without a paddy field, I live on a broken inkstone."

Chapter 2 Beginnings (1864-1870)

During the years 1864 to 65 when I was between two and three, I was the constant concern of my parents and grandparents, owing to my bad health. We were also too poor to afford the sort of medicine prescribed by my doctors and so had to ask for credit from the herbalists. We were all very superstitious. Two days out of three, my grandmother and my mother would go to a nearby temple and prayed for my health. They kowtowed and knocked their heads against the floor until their forehead became swollen like a big persimmon. There were also witch-doctors in my village and my grandmother and mother would get them to come, but my poor health persisted in spite of everything. Somehow, as I grew older, my health improved and in the Winter of the 5th year of Tùng Ch ih (1866), when I was four, I completely recovered.

The Seal: "Ah Chih."

My grandfather often carried me in his arms and played with me. He had a black coat made of goat's fur. It was in a rather poor condition but that was his best article of worldly possession. In Winter, he would tuck me inside his great coat and when I fell asleep, he would hug me very firmly. He always said that having a grandson sleeping close to his chest was the happiest thing in his life. He was fifty-nine then. When the weather was very cold, he would carry me in his arms sitting near a fire and he would use a poker to write my name "Chih" on the ashes. He would say, "This is your name Chih, look at it and don't forget." To tell the truth, my grandfather's vocabulary was very limited, not more than, say, three hundred, and he only half understood some of them. But the word "Chih" he knew quite well. My grandfather would, at intervals of two or three days, teach me one new word and then review the old ones. I was not too dull and I soon remembered all the words he taught me.

During the years 1867-69 my only tutor was my grandfather. Using a pine branch as pen, I would trace out characters on the ground. Sometimes they looked quite all right to me. Sometimes I would draw pictures of heads with round eyes, broad jaws, somewhat like the fat neighbour next door; and when I added a beard to a face, it would look like the cashier of the little store across the street. When I was six years old, a certain district officer of Huang Mao Tui Tsu paid a visit to our village. How he got promoted was not known, but in those days anyone could buy an official position by paying a few hundred taels of silver. There was a lot of fanfare on the day of his arrival and our village people turned out in force to have a look at the new official . My mother asked me whether I wanted to go too and I said quite peremptorily, "I don't want to go." My mother said to me afterwards, "You are quite right. What's the point of going to see the official? We depend on our two hands for our livelihood. What has an official to do with us?"

When I was seven, my grandfather had exhausted his vocabulary and so he repeated and repeated the characters he had taught me and in time I became very familiar with them. In the last month of that year, my grandfather said, "Well, let's have our holiday earlier this year." He was full of praise for me for knowing so many words. On one occasion, after saying that he was glad about my intelligence, he heaved a sigh as if there was something in his mind. My mother understood why my grandfather sighed, which was because he was unable to afford sending me to school to continue my study, and she said to my grandfather, "I have saved a little money which I deposited with a silversmith over the hill. I intended to save a bit more so that I could get a pair of gold hairpins for myself, but I have changed my mind. Why not let me get the money back and buy some paper and books for Ah Chih so that he could study with my father next year? That money will probably be enough for a year's tuition. After that, he can read a bit and be able to write letters and do some bookkeeping." And so it was decided there and then that I should go to school next year, to the great joy of my grandfather.

Thus, at the age of eight, I started going to the little school in Feng Lin T'ing on a hill-slope to the north of Pai Shih P'u about three *li* from my home. My mother made me a blue jacket. Worn over my old black quilted gown, it made me look quite well-dressed. At the school the first thing I did was to kowtow before a commemorative tablet of Confucius, and then afterwards kowtow to my maternal-grandfather, who was to be my tutor. Of course I did not have to pay tuition. My grandfather took me to school in the morning and back home in the evening. Although three *li* was not a long journey, the road was full of mud. It was not too bad on ordinary days, but when rain came it was terrible. Yellow mud is extremely slippery and if you are not careful, you will fall. My grandfather usually carried an umbrella in his right hand and a rice basket in the other, and when the road was really bad he would carry me on his back. In school I was taught the *Three Character Classic*, the *One Hundred Surnames* and the *"Four Character Phrase Book."* Since I already knew some three hundred characters, I found everything quite easy and I was one of the best in the class. Soon I was taught the *Poems by a Thousand Authors* and I found it quite enjoyable. The more I read it, the more I liked it. Although I could recite many of the poems, I could understand only half of them. My favourite ones were always on my lips.

In those days, studying means learning by rote. There was what we called "backing the book" which means that the pupil recites passages with his back to the book, fluently and without hesitation. Calligraphy was also an important part of the

10

curriculum. What my maternal-grandfather taught me was first to trace out characters from a copy-book printed in red by the woodblock process. Compared to writing with a pine branch on the ground, this was a great improvement. My grandfather presented to me a broken ink-stick and a cracked ink-stone. These he had treasured for a long time and were the only items of the "four treasures of the study" in his possession. He had saved these for his own use, to keep accounts, and he seldom took them out. So, with a new brush and some copy paper, the "four treasures" were complete. It was a happy day for me and from then on I spent a lot of time tracing, tracing, tracing. I got somewhat tired of the routine and started to draw.

It happened that over the doors of my neighbour was hung a picture of the Thunder God. It was customary for a family with a new born baby to hang such a picture on the wall, to dispel ghosts and evil spirits. It was rather coarsely done, with red ink on yellow paper, probably by some village painter. When my second brother was born, we had the same sort of painting on the wall and I was quite familiar with it. The more I looked at the picture, the more I wanted to imitate the drawing. So, after school one day, I took out my brush and ink-stone and started to draw. It was a poor effort. The Thunder God that I drew looked more like a funny parrot and so I tried and tried again, but still I could not get the likeness. So I took a sheet of used translucent bamboo paper, put it over the painting on the wall and started to trace the picture. This time it was different. It was so good that I had to do another for one of my classmates. From then on my interest in drawing grew. Because my classmates talked about it, other students came to ask for my drawings. I had often to tear sheets from my exercise books and use them to draw pictures for them. I first started to draw old fishermen. It was not easy and I had to try and try. Then I drew flowers, plants, birds, animals, insects, fishes, cows, horses, pigs, sheep, fowls, shrimps, crabs, frogs, sparrows, butterflies, dragonflies and so on—all the things that I used to see. These are the things I loved best. Nobody ever saw a Thunder God, and so however hard I tried to draw him, the results were always disappointing.

In that year my mother gave birth to my third brother Shun Tsao and as usual, the Thunder God was hung, but this time I did not draw it. I liked to draw for my classmates things that I saw around me and I did this quite often, using up a lot of paper. My maternal-grandfather was familiar with the "Family Mottoes" of Chu Po Lu and he often mumbled something like this, "We must constantly remember that every bowl of rice or congee is not easy to come by; we must keep in mind that every thread and strand of silk is precious material." which are two well-known sayings in that book. When he saw me using up so much paper on such a useless pursuit as drawing, he used to reprimand me with: "You're only playing and not engaged in proper business. Look, how much good paper you have wasted." School children in those days were afraid of their teachers, especially his inevitable ruler, which was often used to beat on their outstretched palms. I was not normally mischievous and seldom had to suffer the indignity of being beaten with a ruler. Once or twice my maternal-grandfather was angry with me for using too much paper, but being very fond of me and in view of my being quite a hardworking boy, I never suffered the usual punishment. In any case, I was so addicted to drawing that it would be quite impossible for me to give it up, and so, in order to avoid spending money on paper, I searched everywhere for used wrapping paper. Autumn came, and I was studying the Confucian Analects when my mother called me to her and said, "It's a bad year and there is not enough money for you to carry on this year's study." I had then to stop studying. We kept ourselves alive by eating yam which my mother taught me to cook over a cow-dung fire. After digging up all the yam we went for wild vegetables. In later years, every time I drew a yam I always thought about the circumstances of those times. I once wrote: "What can conquer my hunger is worth more than half a year of stored food. When I am successful, I should not forget how well it tasted." The sufferings of the poor can only be understood by the poor themselves. It cannot be communicated to the rich.

The Seal: "Bell-wearer."

To Lao She

"I despise people who blandish
 names
Of great artists like Ching and
 Kwan.
Of their boastful partisan
 ways
I am quite ashamed. Strong
Is my sense of nature
Nurtured by the hills
Of Kweilin, often and long.
At the call of the pines I took
 my cane
And went to yonder river-bank
Where the snow was thawing
 and a spring breeze blew:
Imagining myself the legendary
 master Yeh
Trembling at the sight of a
 dragan by the water's brink."

Chapter 3 From Wood-cutting and Cow-herding to Carpentering (1871-77)

During the years 1871-73 I stayed at home help-ing out in carrying water, tending to household affairs, planting vegetables and generally taking care of my two younger brothers. The most important work I did was to gather firewood for fuel. When there was a surplus, we sold it. I was not being idle. What I liked most was cutting firewood. Children in the neighbourhood would go with me up the hills and then after gathering enough firewood, we would take a rest and some of us would play games using little bundles of firewood. We would each take out a bundle, stand them on the ground so that the top end of each bundle would recline against the others like a pyramid. Each of us would

The Seal: "When I was young I hung my books on a buffalo's horns."

in turn throw a length of firewood from a distance against the bundle. Whoever succeeded in demolishing the pyramid won and the stake was usually a bundle of firewood. In this way we could spend enjoyably a good part of the afternoon.

Whenever I had any time I would review the few books that my maternal-grandfather taught me. I also practised calligraphy. As for drawing, this I did only secretly. I would not any more tear paper from my exercise books but used paper from old account books.

When I was eleven, my grandfather rented several *mou* of rice-field and reared a buffalo. So every day I cut wood, took care of the buffalo and at the same time looked after my second brother so that he did not have to be in my mother's way. My health was not good at all and a fortune teller had said about me: "The child is under the influence of the planet Mercury. To avoid calamity, something must be done to ward off its influence." So my grandmother bought me a bronze bell and tied it round my neck with a red string and said to me, "Ah Chih, you take your second brother up the hill and take good care of the buffalo, cut some wood and when dusk falls, I will wait for you at the door. When I hear the bell, I shall know you are coming back and I'll get your dinner ready." My mother also bought a bronze plaquette to serve as good-luck charm, on which was engraved the name of Amitabha Buddha and tied it together with the bell. She said, "With this charm, tigers and leopards and ghosts and spirits up the hills will not dare to come near you." I regret to say that these two ornaments were lost during the civil war in the 1910's. But later on I specially made replicas of them and hanged them on my belt. I also made a seal engraved with the characters "Bell-Hanger" and wrote the following poem on a painting of a buffalo:

Round Star Pond apricot blossoms perfumed the air;
I took a yellow buffalo and walked towards the east.
I had a bell on me, my kind mother's idea;
Now I am myself a bell-listening old man.

I always took some books with me when I went up the hills so as to relieve much of the tedium of looking after the buffalo, picking up cow-dung and cutting firewood. One day I was concentrating on some passages and forgot about everything else, so that when it was time to go home I realised I had gathered very little firewood. After dinner when I was taking my brush out to practise writing, my grandmother said to me, "Ah Chih, your father is my only son; you're my eldest grandson. You are as precious to us as a pearl that glows at night. We thought that our family has added a good helping hand. When you were small and weak, your mother and I were extremely worried for you, burning incense, praying all the time. Now when we lack firewood at home, you would only spend time practising hand-writing and not doing anything useful. We all know the saying: 'After three days of wind and four days of rain, can good literature be boiled in the pot and served as food?' If we do not have rice tomorrow, Ah Chih, what do you propose to do? You mean to say you can fill your stomach with a book and a brush? It is a pity that you were born into the wrong kind of family."

I knew that it was out of good intention that my grandmother said this, hoping that I would thereby make more efforts to help our poor family. From then on, although I still brought along some books whenever I went up the hills, I would hang them on the buffalo's horn and not touch them until I had picked enough dung and cut enough firewood. When I was in school, I had not finished reading the Confucian Analects. Whenever I had the chance, I would make a detour, stop at my maternal grandfather's place and resolve my difficulties with him.

It was customary in our village for children to be "married" when very young; that is, the girl came and lived in the boy's family after a simple ceremony which included making obeisances to the ancestors and heads of the family. Normally, the girl would be slightly older than the boy, so that she could already start doing some housework. It was in a sense a betrothal. It was not until the boy and the girl became adults that they really lived together. The girl was called "child foster-daughter-in-law." This happened usually when the girl's family was poor and was glad to have her taken care of by someone as early as possible. Thus, in the year 1874 when I was twelve, on the 21st day of the first month, I was "married" to a girl called Ch'en Ch'un Chun. She was my senior by one year and being used to housework she was a great help and was often praised by my grandparents. I was quite happy but I never showed it because it was not proper to do so. Thus, she and I contented ourselves by throwing silent glances at one another.

In the same year my grandfather died. When I thought about him, teaching me to write with a pine branch, keeping me warm in his black goat-skin overcoat, taking me to school—all these memories rushed forth and I couldn't stop my tears. I cried for three days and nights. I could not eat anything. My grandmother was crying hard too, but when she saw me in such a condition, she said, "Don't cry so hard; you're weak and your grandfather wouldn't like to see you so run down." My father and mother also tried to stop me from crying, but I could not control myself. This was the first misfortune that happened to me. We had very little money then, only sixty silver *yuan*, but we managed to give my grandfather a dignified funeral.

During the years 1875-76, we were not doing too well. There was only my father to take care of the farm and it was a great strain on him. My mother always said this to me, "Ah Chih, I only wish you had grown-up brothers to help your father support the family." In our village, we used firewood for fuel and in the Summer of the year when I was thirteen, there was plenty of rain so that I was unable to go up the hills for firewood. Sometimes when we ran out of rice, we would dig up some wild vegetable and bake it, using dried cow-dung for fuel. Sometimes when the stove had not been used for some time, the rain-water that had seeped in would remain there, a good breeding ground for frogs.

When I was fourteen, my mother gave birth to my fourth brother Shun Pei and for some months, my wife helped to take care of the baby. As I have said, my health was poor and other than picking firewood and cow-dung, taking care of the buffalo, doing some odd jobs at home, I never did anything

19

in the fields. So, one day my father said to me, "You're not too young to learn some farming now." Then he taught me the use of the plough. For many days I was struggling hard, being unable to control the plough nor the buffalo. My father also taught me how to sow seeds and this caused more fatigue. I had to bend my back all day long with my feet soaked in water. On one occasion, after a day's work, I was washing my feet when suddenly I felt a sharp pain on one of my feet as if inflicted by a pair of pincers. I saw blood coming out from one of my toes. I heard my father say, "It's a grass-shrimp that has bitten my boy."

When I was fifteen (1877), my father realised that I was not fit to be a farm-worker. He considered sending me away to learn a handicraft. It occurred that one of our relatives, a carpenter, visited us during the New Year festival and during dinner, my father persuaded him to take me on as an apprentice. So it came to pass that after some ceremony I was officially accepted as an apprentice. My instructor was a so-called "large-wood craftsman," that is, doing all kinds of coarse structures like building the frame of a hut, ordinary tables and beds, and so on. The real test came when my instructor took me to a building site, and I found to my distress that I was not strong enough and could not carry large logs. So after sometime, my instructor decided that I should not continue being a carpenter's apprentice. My father got another instructor for me. He was named Ch'i Ch'ang Ling, a very considerate person. He often said, "If you go on doing it, you will be able to do it." I remember one day when he and I had finished work on a building site and three persons who looked like carpenters were walking towards us. Since they were all carpenters, I did not take too much notice of them. But to my surprise, when they came near us, my instructor stood at attention and smiling with his hands down, bowed to them. The three only nodded acknowledgement, in a rather haughty manner. When they had left, I asked my instructor why he behaved so humbly towards them since we were all carpenters, to which he replied, "Child, you don't know courtesy. We are craftsmen of coarse articles, but they are craftsmen of refined ones. They can carve and make artistic things. Unless you're clever, you just can't do it. How can we compare ourselves to them." From that day on I made up my mind to be a "small-wood craftsman."

The Seal: Boy with buffalo.

"This I painted when I was twenty and now I am over ninety. Between these years, there have been many changes in my technique and style, and this gives rise to many expressions of astonishment and regret."

The Seal: "I am a common person, common as grass and plants."

Chapter 4 From Flower-carver to Painter, 1878-1889

In 1878 when I was sixteen, my grandmother and my mother, considering that my health had disqualified me as a carpenter, discussed the matter with my father in the hope that he would agree to let me change to another line of business. So I expressed my wish to be a "small-wood craftsman" and my father very quickly succeeded in persuading a certain flower-carver called Chou Chih Mei to take me on as an apprentice. He was thirty-eight and was well-known in the trade as an expert carver. He was particularly good at carving figures. We got on extremely well. I admired his talent and was interested in learning his craft. He thought I was intelligent and a good apprentice and, as he had no children, he treated me like a son. He went so far as to say to others, "This apprentice of mine

The Seal: "Student of Lu Pan."
      (Note: Lu Pan was the God of Carpentry.)

23

will get somewhere in the future and I shouldn't be surprised that he will become famous one day and I shall feel honoured for having taught him something." People thought me promising too and I could never forget the goodwill my instructor cherished towards me. When I was seventeen, I suffered a serious ailment, coughing blood several times. I was on the brink of death. Needless to say, my parents were extremely concerned about me. My mother had just given birth to my fifth brother Shun Chun and she felt quite helpless. Fortunately, a certain herbalist called Chang came to my rescue, but I had lost considerable time in my apprenticeship. It was customary for the duration of apprenticeship to be a little over three years, but because of my illness, that had to be prolonged. However, I finally graduated. This was a great event and my family celebrated it by inviting several dozen people to dinner. This happened just when Ch'un Chun and I became husband and wife in fact, not in name only. She was now twenty and I well over nineteen. Although I had completed my apprenticeship, I still attached myself to instructor Chou and served as his assistant. It did not take long for my name to be known a hundred miles around my village. People called me Wood-worker Chih and sometimes even Master Chih when they felt inclined to be polite towards me. My family was still not well off and so I gave my mother all the money I earned. My instructor and I often went to work in the home of Ch'i Pe Ch'ang and I got to know his son Kung Fu. We both became good friends.

In those days, flower-carvers were fond of using

traditional subjects like flower basket, unicorn, plum, peach and so on. I always thought that variety was essential in art. I drew grapes, pomegranates, plums, peaches, pears, apricots, peonies, plum flowers, orchids, bamboos, chrysanthemums and so on. For figures, I used subjects from novels and historical anecdotes. This at once became popular and I was greatly encouraged. But my family's economic conditions were still far from being good, although I managed to make more money by now. My wife Ch'un Chun was very hard-working and she never complained. When our neighbours asked how she was doing, she always said, "Very well." But it was difficult to hide things from our neighbours and on one occasion, a woman next door said to my wife provocatively, "Why do you want to suffer poverty here. With your ability, would there be any difficulty finding a wealthier husband?" But Ch'un Chun, smiling, replied, "I know my deserts. There is no need for you to plan on my behalf." When I was twenty, I came by chance upon a copy of *The Mustardseed Garden, a Handbook of Painting*, printed in five colours in the reign of Ch'ien Lung. Although it was not a complete set, I was able to follow its instructions and use it as a guide. Only then did I realise that what I had been drawing were far from being accurate. So I started all over again. Since the book was not mine and I could not afford to buy another set, I spent half a year tracing out all the pictures and ever since then I had been using specimens from the book as models for my carvings.

What I earned from my carvings was still not sufficient to maintain my family. My mother was still worrying about "the seven matters upon opening the door*" and my grandmother often denied herself food in order to give it to me. I could not look at the situation without making some efforts to improve it. So I spent a lot of my evenings making carvings and on the following morning took them to the shops in White Stone Market for sale on consignment. I made tobacco boxes, using buffalo horn. It was quite popular. I could produce one every two or three evenings and after deducting the twenty per cent commission, I could buy a peck of rice with the proceeds. Smoking was already in vogue in those days and I had early developed a taste for tobacco. There were two types of tobacco smoking. One was "han yen", dry-smoking, using the whole leaf, and the other kind is "shui yen," wet-smoking, using shredded leaves in a water pipe. I smoked both kinds. Now that my tobacco boxes were finding a market, I could afford to indulge in the luxury. When I was twenty-one (1883), Ch'un Chun had her first pregnancy. In spite of her condition, when we had used up our firewood at home, she had to go up the hill at the back of our hut to get firewood. It was a very strenuous climb. When her pregnancy was at an advanced stage, she sometimes had to crawl going up the hill. Our first child was a girl and we gave her the name Chu ju.

Between 1884 and 1888, I carried on as a flower-carver, meanwhile making tobacco boxes as a side-line. Ever since I made a copy of the *Mustardseed Garden,* I had painted every one of those pictures several times over. I was quite an adept and my name soon spread. I was often paid for my paintings

* They are firewood, rice, oil, sugar, sauce, vinegar and salt.

although sometimes I received presents instead. The name Carpenter Chih was always associated with painting. I used to say, "One should speak a language that people can understand, and paint things that people can see." The Thunder Gods that I used to paint I now considered unworthy of my art. After all, the Thunder God was a fictitious figure. I preferred painting figures in old costumes because they were actually worn by the ancients and were illustrated in the *Mustardseed Garden*. After seeing an opera I would draw figures in constumes used in the opera. I was quite well-known in my village now. Most people asked me to paint pictures of gods such as the Jade Emperor, Lao Tzu, God of Fortune, God of the Kitchen, Yama, the Dragon God, the Thunder God, God of Lightning, the Rain God, the Wind God, Cow-Head, Horse-Face, the Four Guardians of Buddhist Temples, Door Gods, and so on. Although I did not like drawing these things, I did it for the sake of the fees which were one thousand coins per picture. Of course I sometimes painted to please my village relatives or friends. Sometimes my drawings were benevolent-looking figures, using pictures from the *Mustardseed Garden* as models, but it was difficult to draw fierce-looking figures. It won't do to make all figures look like the Thunder God! So I used some extraordinary looking persons among members of my circle as models and when I had finished the pictures, I was often amused at the results

By the time I was twenty-six I had five brothers and three sisters and my family consisted of fourteen members. We were all busy working, some of us tending the fields, some picking firewood and others taking care of the buffalo. My grandmother was now seventy-seven and all she could do was to watch the young children play. Besides looking after the poultry and watering the vegetables, Ch'un Chun helped my mother to weave. She would sit under the shade of a vine-lattice weaving. I was often away from home and when I came back I was often a little annoyed by the monotonous sound of the shuttle. When I think of it now, the sound was rather sweet and I am somewhat nostalgic about it. Many years after, I wrote a poem about this:

My wife laughed at me for wasting my life
Always travelling abroad in bad health and times.
The sound of weaving from underneath the vine's shade—
I loathed it then but yearn now to hear it again.

At this juncture I must record my indebtedness to someone called Hsiao Hsiang Kai, an accomplished painter, although by profession a paper-craft artist. I owed my first lessons to this sanguine man. It was when I was twenty-seven (1889) that I first met Mr. Hu Ch'in Yuan who came to see me for a picture. He was impressed with my skill and one day he asked me earnestly, "Do you want to start studying as well as learning to paint?" to which I replied, "I do want to study and paint, but I am too poor to be able to afford it." He said, "Don't worry, as long as you have the will, you can study and sell pictures at the same time. Come and see me when you are free."

Mr. Hu Ch'in Yuan was a generous, straight-forward and amiable person. He was a collector as well as an accomplished painter, calligrapher and poet. He often invited friends to his home, making verses together. "Round the table there are always many guests; inside the bottle there is no lack of wine." So, one day I called on him. He was entertaining friends, but glad to see me. He invited me to stay for lunch and presented me to the private tutor employed by his family, called Ch'en Tso Hsun, a well-known scholar of Hsiang T'an. Mr. Hu said to me during lunch, "If you want to study you can call Mr. Chen your tutor right now, but what would your parents say?" I said, "My parents will of course respect your wish, but unfortunately we are too poor. . . . ." at which Mr. Hu interrupted me, "Didn't I tell you that you can sell your paintings to support your family? Your paintings are saleable, so don't worry." I said, "But I am afraid I am too old and it's too late." Mr. Hu said, "Haven't you read the Three Character Classic? There it says:

Su Lao Ch'uan
At twenty-seven
Began serious studies.

You're now exactly twenty-seven, why don't you learn from Su Lao Ch'uan?" Mr. Ch'en took up the conversation and said, "If you really want to study I shall waive your tuition fee." All the others at the table spoke to the effect that since I could study under the expert guidance of Mr. Chen and learn painting from Mr. Hu, I need not worry about remaining obscure. When I told Mr. Hu that I was eternally grateful to him for his generosity, he said, "Quit calling me Mr. Hu. Just call me teacher." So the matter was decided there and then. After lunch, as custom would have it, I made the usual obeisences before a commemorative tablet of Confucious and forthwith became a student of Mr. Hu and Mr. Ch'en.

I settled down in the Hu family. My instructors gave me the name Huang and the fancy name Pin Sheng. Because I lived near the White Stone Village, I was called White Stone Hermit. The last was used as signature on my paintings. Mr. Chen said to me one day, "It is always best to be able to write poems so that you can put them on your paintings. Go and study the *Three Hundred T'ang Poems*. This book is enjoyed by all, both the learned and ordinary people. It is commonly said that even the uninitiated will be able to make poetry if they know the *Three Hundred T'ang Poems* by heart." I knew the volume called *Poems by One Thousand Authors* when I was young and so I was able to enjoy the *Three Hundred T'ang Poems* like meeting old friends. After two months, Mr. Chen asked me, "How many poems do you know now by heart?" and when I told him that I knew almost all the three hundred T'ang poems, he was somewhat skeptical. But when he took some poems at random and examined me on them, he was convinced that I told the truth. From there I proceeded to study *Mencius* and as a kind of recreation I read *The Strange Stories of a Chinese Studio* and the *Essays of the Eight Masters of T'ang and Sung*. I found reading the greatest pleasure in life. I had then started to draw flowers, birds, grass and insects. Mr. Hu always told me this, "Stones should be lean, trees should be curved, birds should live and your hands should be practised." He let me study his collection of paintings and calligraphy. He also

30

introduced me to one T'an Li Sheng and wanted me to study landscape painting with him. Mr. Hu would often inscribe my paintings with poems of his and was fond of telling me, "Go and study poetry. It would be a pity not to be able to inscribe poems on your paintings."

It was Spring, the waterlilies were blossoming. Mr. Hu's friends were all making poems and they invited me to take part. So I plucked up courage and presently completed a seven-character quatrain. My heart pounded fast and I was afraid I had made a fool of myself. But Mr. Hu, smiling, said of my poem, "Not bad, not bad," at the same time reading it aloud. Everyone thought I had great talent and I was glad that this first shot of mine made an impact.

In the same year my first son was born and we called him Liang Yuan. Living with the Hu family was most pleasant. I was making good income out of my drawings. Photography was not yet common and I was doing good business portraying the rich. For every portrait, I received two taels of silver. That was not bad. From that time onwards I put aside the chisel and took up the writing-brush instead. Between the age of twenty-eight and thirty-two, I depended on drawing for my living. Although I was much better off than before, I often went to bed groping in the dark for lack of oil for the lamp. Sometimes I had no light except that from burning pinewood and did a lot of reading this way. I distinctly remembered I read the Po Chu-I volume called *Ch'ang Ch'ing Chi* in this manner. When I was seventy, I wrote a poem entitled "To my Children Recalling Past Events," which describes this episode:

In my poor village I started learning very late,
And never seriously studied till I was twenty-seven.
What harm was there, not having oil for fuel?
I used to burn pine branches and read T'ang poetry.

Chapter 5 Fame comes slowly

At thirty (1892), my painting business expanded as I became better-known. My mother's knitted brows began to relax and my grandmother once said to me, smiling, "Ah Chih, you haven't done injustice to your writing-brush. I used to say that you couldn't cook a meal with books, but now I can see that you can with your paintings." I began to extend my activities into landscape painting, flowers, birds and so on, besides portraiture. The women especially wanted me to draw historical figures like Mu Lan and Wen Chi. Those figures pleased them so much that they jokingly called me Ch'i The Beautiful. In fact, my drawings were far from perfect, but there was no competition around. There were, however, a few snobs who would ask me to paint, but did not want me to inscribe my

The seal: "Kitchen for cooking pictures"

name on the pictures because they thought I did not belong to the elite. I thought this was ridiculous. However, since they paid, I thought nothing of it. In the same year, I learned the art of mounting pictures.

I had begun to join a poetry group. My friends' poems were usually rather formal, full of classical allusions and clever rhymes, but not always inspired. I believe that poetry should be concerned with the spirit and although form is important, it is the spirit that gives poetry life. Thus, although I did not have the skill of my friends, my poems were not necessarily less pleasing. The group had no fixed days for meeting. We gathered together and talked about poetry and literature in general and sometimes calligraphy, painting, seal-engraving as well as song-writing. We had borrowed some rooms in a monastery in Five-Dragon Hill and we called our group the Dragon Hill Poetry Society. It was a quiet well-wooded retreat, a kind of summer resort. The nucleus of the Society consisted of Wang Chung Yen, Lo Chen Wu, Lo Hsing Wu, Chen Fu Ken, T'an Tsu Ch'uan, Hu Li San and myself. People called us The Seven Scholars of Dragon Hill. They all wanted me to be president of the Society. At first I resisted the idea because as far as learning and social position were concerned, I was much their inferior. I thought they were pulling my leg , but when Wang Chung Yen said, "Don't be stubborn. You're the oldest amongst us. If you will not take up the job, who will? Don't stand on ceremony any more." Against this I had no defence.

Soon another poetry society was formed meeting in Li Sung An's place and was called the Lo Shan

Poetry Society. Lo Shan and Dragon Hill were about fifty *li* apart and in spite of the distance, many of us of Dragon Hill also joined the Lo Shan. When I was thirty-three (1895), drought hit our village. There was impending famine and the poorer villagers flocked to the wealthy families for meals. In those days, rich families always had their granaries well stocked and it was customary for the poor in days of difficulty to line up outside their doors, usually in an orderly manner, to ask for food. They would do their cooking there and were in general considerate enough to go away after several meals and seek help elsewhere. But other groups would arrive. Since we sometimes turned out in force to attend poetry meetings at the Li family, people sometimes wondered why we self-proclaimed poets should join the refugee ranks.

My presence at both poetry societies was particularly welcomed, one of the reasons being that I could make hand-painted letter paper. This was used for poetry writing. White paper did not seem good enough to write poems on. Very often I spent nights drawing flowers, birds, fishes, shrimps and landscape on letter-sized sheets for the benefit of my friends. They were not unappreciative and I have heard one of them say that since I had to spend evenings doing those paintings, the paper should be carefully used and preserved.

When I was thirty-four (1896) I began to take up calligraphy seriously. At first I practised the court style, that is, the formal type of writing used in court examinations. My two instructors wrote in the style of Ho Shao Chi and I had for some time followed their example. I once had a rather humiliating experience. I had asked someone from Ch'ang Sha reputed to be a good seal-engraver to do a seal for me, on a piece of Shou Shan stone. After a few days I went to see if it was done, but he returned the stone to me, saying, "Polish it first before I'll do it." I looked at the piece of stone and found it to be as smooth as could be, but since he demanded it, I polished it again and took it back to him. He did not so much as look at the stone but put it aside. So after a few days I went to see him again and he handed me back the stone, saying, "It is not smooth enough, take it back and polish it." He was indeed arrogant and I am sure he did not think much of the piece of stone or myself. I thought, "Why should I suffer all this just for a seal!" So I took the stone back, and in the same evening, I did the engraving myself. When my host saw the stone next morning, he told me that my engraving showed more elegance than any done by the visitor from Ch'ang Sha. I felt flattered as I knew I had little idea of engraving. From that day on, I practised real hard. I remembered particularly the advice of a skillful practitioner called Li T'ieh An, who said, "There is a lot of good stone in this area. Carry a whole basketful home and start to engrave and erase, engrave and erase. When you have filled three or four *tien hsin** boxes, you will have achieved something."

I never travelled more than a hundred *li* from Apricot Valley until I was thirty-five, when a friend asked me to go to the city to do a portrait.

When I was thirty-seven, I was introduced to Mr. Wang Hsiang Ch'i, a famous artist, by Mr. Chang Chung Yang. I submitted some of my poems,

*General name for pastries, cookies, tarts etc.

paintings, seals and specimens of calligraphy for him to look at, and he said, "Your paintings and seal-engravings are remarkably like those of the monk Chi Shan." I felt greatly encouraged because Chi Shan was an accomplished artist, a descendant of the Sung poet Huang Shan Ku. To be compared to him was no mean honour, all the more so when the opinion was given by Wang Hsiang Ch'i. A lot of people claimed to be students of his because that would raise their prestige, but I had resisted several times being introduced to him because I was afraid people might think I was trying to boost myself. Wang Hsiang Ch'i did not realise that and was known to have said to someone, "Everyone has his own peculiar temperament. There is a bronze craftsman of Heng Yang named Ts eng Chao Chi and the iron craftsman of Wu Shih Chai, Chang Chung Yang, and there is also this carpenter who is very industrious but never wanted to be my student." When Chang Chung Yang heard this, he came especially to acquaint me of it. He said, "Since Mr. Wang think so highly of you, why don't you go and seek his instructions. A lot of people wanted to be his students, but never succeeded. Why do you play hard-to-get?" I was in fact grateful for Mr. Wang's sentiment towards me and so I plucked up courage and on the eighteenth of the tenth month, I went with Chang Chung Yang to see him and officially became his student. But I felt that I was too uncouth   and was always conscious that people might criticise me for being a climber. So I never dared to mention Mr. Wang's name in front of people, but I admired Mr. Wang very deeply. Chang Chung Yang once told me, "Our master thinks that your prose is quite presentable, but your poetry reads like Hsieh P'an of the Red Chamber Dream." That hit the nail on the head because I wrote what my heart commands without putting on too much embellishment and indeed my poetry somewhat resembles that character. About that time I engraved more than ten seals for some well-known members of the gentry, the T'an brothers, the eldest being T'an Yen K'ai. A certain Scholar Ting, a self-styled expert in seal-engraving spoke derogatively of me to the T'an brothers. They accordingly erased my engravings and instead invited Scholar Ting to do them all over again. When I heard about this, I said to myself, "Ting and I both took after the style of Ting Lung Hung and Huang Hsiao Sung. How can his engraving be right and mine wrong." But I was sure sooner or later I would be vindicated and so I thought no more of it.

When I was thirty-eight, I did a painting for a wealthy salt merchant, who wanted his tour of the seventy-two peaks in Heng Mountains to be permanently recorded. The immensity of the landscape necessitated my making twelve scrolls each measuring six feet in height. In order to please the salt merchant, I used rather heavy colouring, so much so that I used up two catties of a pigment called "stone green" or malachite, to mention nothing else. To me this seemed quite ridiculous, but the salt merchant was very pleased with the result and gave me 320 taels of silver. That was a lot of money and people were greatly impressed by this. My prestige as a painter was greatly enhanced and demand for my paintings grew rapidly.

With the money I was able to move to Mei Kung Shrine. Here I could see many plum trees all around and so I called my abode "The Hundred Plum Book House." I built a small study and called it "Borrowed Hill Poetry Chamber" and planted some banana trees around it. In Summer the banana trees gave good shade and in Autumn, during rainy nights, the rustling of the banana leaves gave rise to poetic thoughts. Here in this chamber, I wrote several hundred poems.

Mei Kung Shrine was not far from Star Pond and so Ch'un Chun and I often exchanged visits with my parents. There were many lily ponds along the way, and during blossom time the perfume from the flowers was enchanting. I planted many lilies too in front of my house. Because the seed-pockets of the lilies attracted intruders, I built a little shed with hay and my two sons were ordered to keep watch there by turn. My elder son was twelve and the younger six. Ordinarily they would go up the hills to pick firewood and I was very glad they were hardworkers. One day, just after noon, I took a stroll by the pond and saw my younger son lying inside the shed which was so small it could hardly cover his whole length. He was fast asleep and his old clothes were wet through with sweat. I looked at the grass underneath and it was all dried up by the scorching sun. How could he stand the cruel heat, I thought, and he was so young. So I called him, "Liang Fu, are you asleep?" He sat up and looked sheepishly at me, afraid that I might scold him for taking a siesta. He was glad I ordered him to go back to the house.

1901: I was thirty-nine. Someone asked me why I used Borrowed Hill to name my house. I said, "That is simple enough. The hill is not mine. I borrowed it to please myself." To commemorate the occasion I painted a picture of "The Borrowed-Hill Poetry Chamber." In the same year, my grandmother died. When I thought about our poorer days and how she starved herself in order to save enough food for me, I felt as if my heart was being pierced by a knife.

The Seal: "Poverty improves poetry."

Chapter 6 Five Trips

1902: I was forty. My third child was born. Hitherto, I had not travelled far from my old village. I was not ambitious and all I wanted in those days was to make enough to keep the wolf from the door. In the Autumn of that year I was invited by Hsia Wu I to go to Sian to teach his mistress Yao Wu Shuang the art of painting. All travelling expenses having been remitted to me, I was hesitating between accepting the invitation or not, when my friend Kuo Pao Sheng who was also in Sian wrote me a long letter persuading me to take the trip. The letter said, "Whether you write prose or poetry, paint or engrave, you will improve with travelling. This is especially true of painting. You must train your power of observation. The ancient phrase 'aided by mountains and rivers'

The Seal: "Enjoying the view of the Western Mountains to my heart's content."

applies to this. To copy painters of the past will get you nowhere. If you travel often, your horizons will be widened, your sympathies more universal and, coupled with your own artistic gifts, your prospects will be unlimited. Capture the great scenic spots and put them down on paper and you will have many masterpieces. I realise your indecision is due to your family responsibilities, but for the sake of your art, you should come to Sian. Do start quickly and not hesitate." I had a discussion with my parents and having obtained their agreement I went on the journey.

It was a slow and long journey but it afforded many opportunities to paint. I then realised why masters of the past painted the way they did.

In Sian I was introduced to the well-known official and poet Fan Tseng Hsiang. He was very well-disposed towards me. I engraved many seals for him. I was on several occasions persuaded by Chang Chung Yang to take advantage of the situation and to get an appointment as a government official. I, as always, was never interested in officialdom and I despised social climbers. I was naive enough to reprove Chang for being too ambitious.

When I was forty-one, I took a trip to Peking with Hsia Wu I and his family. Passing through Hua Shan we enjoyed much beautiful scenery. Peach blossoms accompanied us on the way for scores of miles. Having crossed the Yellow River, we could see Sung Shan and the scenery was of a different kind. One day I saw a rectangular piece of stone lying at the bottom of a stream. It was very smooth and I thought I might use it to polish my knives with. When I picked it up I discovered it was a piece of Han Dynasty brick, a relic of the Bronze Bird Terrace. I was overcome with joy. What a pity that this precious object should be looted from me during the civil war.

In Peking, every day I taught Yao Wu Shuang. Otherwise I painted and engraved and sold my paintings and seals. I often went to Liu Li Ch'ang and looked at antiques and things. Sometimes I would go to see operas. I made several friends including one Ts eng Hsi. At first I thought he was one of those bureaucrats who cared for nothing but power. I had instructed the doorman to say "not at home" to him when he called. After several unsuccessful visits, Ts eng one day burst into my room without being announced, crying, "I am here. Can you refuse to see me now?" I am glad to say that he turned out to be a person of considerable learning and I did owe him an apology for misjudging him.

I had long wanted to go home after having saved some money. I did not want to stay in the capital and mix daily with the bureaucrats. When I heard Fan Tseng Hsiang was coming to Peking, I made up my mind to leave immediately for fear he might insist on my taking up an official appointment. I had saved some two thousand silver taels by now and with that I can live quite comfortably in my home village. So before starting on my journey, I ordered sixty painting brushes to be made, each engraved with a serial number and bearing the name "Pai Shih Hsien Sheng.*" I was criticised for using the designation "Hsien Sheng" as being too self-important. But I was only taking after the style of Chin Tung Hsin; and why not?

*an honorific meaning "mister".

43

Fan Tseng Hsiang arrived in Peking soon after I left. When he heard that I had gone, he said to Hsia Wu I, "Ch'i has great nobility of character. But he is a little bit unsociable."

This ended my first long trip. When I was forty-two (1904), Wang Hsiang Ch'i, Chang Chung Yang and I visited Nanchang. After seeing Kiu Kiang and Lu Shan. We stayed at Wang Hsiang Ch'i's. On the seventh of the seventh month, he gave a wine party. He declared during dinner, "Since the departure of Ts eng Kuo Fan, all literary activities have ceased. We should revive them. To commemorate this occasion, how about each of us composing some couplets." Thereupon he recited the "head" part of an unfinished couplet and wanted us to furnish the "tail." We looked at each other helplessly. Sizing up the situation, our host did not insist.

When I thought about the episode upon my returning home, I was filled with shame and regret. Poetry writing is no easy matter—one must first inform oneself with a great deal of learning before one can begin to make poetry. How can I then call myself a poet? So I drop the character Yin (versifying) from the name Chieh Shan Yin Kuan (Borrowed-Hill Poetry Chamber) and call it simply Chieh Shan Kuan.

1905: I was forty-three. I first saw Chao Chih Ch'ien's "*Erh Chin Tieh T'ang Yin P'u*", Seal Engravings of the House of Two Golden Butterflies, in the home of Li Wei Sun. I borrowed and copied it and was quite satisfied with the result. From then on I engraved in the style of Chao. I used to paint in the "*kung pi*" style but ever since Sian I

Note: "Kung pi" — delicate, elaborate style of painting.

44

had dropped it in favour of the "*yi pi*"[*] style. In calligraphy I used to write in the style of Ho Shao Chi but after meeting Li Yun An in Peking, I learned to write in the style of Han Dynasty monuments, which I maintain to this day. People told me that after two trips my paintings, calligraphy and engravings all looked different. Indeed this was the chief turning-point in my artistic life.

In Autumn, I visited Kweilin at the invitation of Wang Sung Nien who was Director of Education there. I was glad I went because the scenery of Kwangsi, of which Kweilin was the capital, was indeed magnificent. There is nothing like it anywhere else. Here I began to open my eyes to the possibilities of landscape painting. But Kweilin's climate was capricious and unpredictable. One has to be prepared for sudden warmth and cold. I wrote a poem on this:

> The weather of Kwangsi is just impossible!
> For a short trip one has to pack a lot of clothes.
> Going through Yang Shuo in a skiff any day,
> Light gauze when the South wind blows but fur when the North.

I was not exaggerating!

In Kweilin, I set up as painter and engraver. When in Sian, Fan Ts'en Hsiang had helped me to work out a scale of fees for my art works. I used his name in this connection and hung up a sign with a scale of fees. I was not surprised when it worked. My business flourished.

Ts'ai O , recently returned from Japan, was head of a police training school. One day, he sent a

The Seal: "I create a tradition of my own."

Note: "yi pi" — a style of painting in which the artist aims primarily to express an idea.

45

deputy to see me, saying, "Students at the police training school create a lot of trouble every time they take leave on Sunday. It would be a great help if Mr. Ch'i would teach them painting on Sundays at a salary of thirty taels per month." The pay was considered very good, but I decided not to accept, saying, "If students create trouble outside school, they can also create trouble in school. If they should succeed in ejecting me, how very embarrassing that would be! It is better for me not to take the job." I was considered a freak for turning down such a good offer.

I met a monk one day at a friend's. He called himself Chang Chung Cheng, but everybody called him Chang the monk. He was rather shifty in his behaviour, never giving a direct answer to people's queries. He had once commissioned me to paint four scrolls and paid me twenty taels of silver. When he knew I was going back to my home village, he came and said, "When are you going? I'll take my horse and see you off." A very friendly monk indeed! The name Huang K'o Ch'iang appeared very often in the newspapers in the early years of the Republic. A friend afterwards asked me, "Do you know Mr. Huang K'o Ch'iang?" I said, "No, I do not." "But you must have met him before," he said. "No, I am afraid I never did." My friend laughed, saying, "Chang the monk whom you met in Kweilin was neither a monk nor surnamed Chang. He was the same Huang K'o Ch'iang." But I never saw this illustrious person again after the first encounter.

1906: I was forty-four. I was going to return home when I received news that my fourth brother

Note: Huang K'o Ch'iang (Huang Hsing) was one of the leaders of the 1911 Revolution.

Shun P'ei and my eldest son Liang Yuan were both in Kwangtung, serving in the army. My family was anxious about them and wanted me to go and see them. I finally traced them to Ch'in Chou where they were under the banner of Kuo Pao Sheng, who, on seeing me, said smiling, "Who would have thought that this should have brought you here!" Kuo Pao Sheng was quite an adept at painting flowers and fishes and I was prevailed upon to stay several months with him, meanwhile teaching his mistress to paint. Kuo was rather vain and was not averse to saying "yes" to those who come to ask for a picture. I was very often his "ghost painter," for which I received good fees. He had collected many paintings of Pa Ta Shan Jen, Hsu Wei, Chin Tung Hsin and others. I lost no time to make good use of them.

I returned home in Autumn and this ended my third long trip.

My teacher Chou Chih Mei died not long after. He had treated me like his own son and spared no pains in imparting to me all his knowledge and skill in flower-carving. He had no children. I wrote a memorial essay on him but how could this little expression of gratitude serve as repayment of the debt that I owed him.

The lease for Mei Kung Shrine expired and I bought and renovated an old house not far away, together with twenty *mou* of paddy field. I called the house Chi P'ing T'ang. It had a study which I called "Eight-Inkstone Chamber" the reason being that I had brought back during my travels eight inkstones. My first grandson was born a month after the moving and I gave him the sobriquet

The seal: "Old man of Apricot Valley"

"Removal Grandson." My neighbours were quick to congratulate me on all the happenings and indeed I was much better off now and feeling better too.

1907: I was forty-five. When I was in Ch'in Chou last year, I had promised Kuo Pao Sheng to return the following year, and so soon after the new year I kept the promise.

Kuo and I toured Ting Hu, Kao Yao, Tuan Chi. We went across Ch'in Chou's border to Vietnam. There the landscape is often adorned with hundreds of wild banana trees which dyed the sky giving it a glorious jade colour. One of my paintings, entitled "Visitor and Green Sky," now collected under *Chieh Shan T'u Chuan*, describes this.

It was lychee season. Clusters upon clusters of red lychees gladdened the eye. That was when lychees first had a place in my pictures. Once someone came with a big basket of lychees and exchanged them for one of my paintings. A song girl to whom I had shown favour often peeled lychees for me. A poem records the episode:

In Ch'in Chou, I dreamt often of home.
On the river at South Gate the rain was falling.
With nimble fingers she peeled lychees for me—
Alas, such homely joy can never be repeated.

I returned home again in Winter. This was the fourth trip.

1908: I was forty-six.

Lo Hsing Wu, who was now an official of the Education Department in Canton, invited me to visit with him. The Cantonese were not too keen on my paintings, their taste being confined to the

"Four-Wang" school. But they were very impressed with my seal-engravings and every day I had at least ten requests for them. So I decided to settle down there for a while.

Lo was a member of Sun Yat Sen's T'ung Meng Hui, working as a secret agent. He was one of the seven members of the Dragon Hill Poetry Society. We were very close and we never hid anything from each other. He persuaded me to help the Revolutionary movement, acting as a courier. It thus transpired that several times a month I was instrumental in transmitting secret messages hidden between paintings. This was never discovered.

I returned home in Autumn and stayed there very briefly before starting out again to fetch my fourth brother and my eldest son home, on the instruction of my father. In the beginning of 1909, when I was forty-seven, having reached Ch'in Chou and stayed there for a few days we passed Canton, took a ship in Hong Kong and headed for Shanghai. From there we went to Soochow, Nanking, and at last reached home, this being the end of my fifth trip.

1910: I was forty-eight.

I was always conscious that I had too little learning and I made up my mind to start all over again. Based on the rough drafts I made during my travels, I did fifty-two paintings under the title Chieh Shan T'u Chuan. I also did twenty-four paintings at the request of Hu Lien Shih using the descriptive titles by Wang Chung Yen based on scenes around the former's residence.

I had by now developed a style of seal-engraving which could be described as a fusion of those of

Han Dynasty and Chao Hui Shu. I was complimented on its mystique and austerity characteristic of the ancients. The T'an brothers, who at the suggestion of one scholar Ting, had erased my work on their stones, returned to have them re-engraved by me. How things changed with circumstances. One of my poems has this: "When fame descends, my temples are white like silk."

1911: I was forty-nine.

When my teacher Wang Hsiang Ch'i visited Changsha, I immediately besought him to compose a memorial biography of my grandmother. This I personally engraved on stone afterwards.

1912: I was fifty.

By now, I had decided not to wander far from my village any more. When I was fifty-one, I bequeathed on my three sons the little saving that I had in the hope that they might be able to launch their own careers with it. At that time my eldest son Liang Yuan was twenty-five, my second son Liang Fu twenty and my third son Liang Kun twelve. The last being too young to fend for himself stayed with us. Although my eldest and second sons were living with us, they were made to be independent and to "maintain separate kitchens." Liang Yuan supported himself without great difficulty, with a job that paid reasonable wages; but Liang Fu depended on hunting for his livelihood and was daily fretting about being poor. On the first day of the tenth month, he fell ill; on the third day he came over, sat near the stove and talked to his mother about his impoverished state. Ch'un Chun and I both thought he was just trying to elicit sympathy from us like all children did and we did not pay much attention to him. Who would have expected just five days later he died. Ch'un Chun wept bitterly and I regretted deeply my haste in making the decision that led to the disaster.

1914: I was fifty-two.

I planted thirty pear trees in front of my house. I was reminded of Su Shih's remark in his letter to Ch'eng Ch'uan Fu, "If planted when too big, it may not grow; if planted too small, old people may not see the fruition." I was afraid I might not live to taste their fruits; but I did, and what pears! Each weighing over a pound, they were sweet as honey.

On the fifth of the fifth month, I sent a letter by messenger to my old teacher Hu Ch'in Yuan only to see the messenger hurrying back with the sad tidings that he had passed away seven days ago. Words could not describe my sorrow. Hu was not only my teacher but also my bosom friend. How could I help feeling a sense of extreme loss and debt unrepaid. I went over my old paintings and took out the ones that he had liked, about twenty of them, mounted them myself, put them in a paper box that I specially made for the purpose and burnt them in front of his coffin. I also wrote this in his memory:

> Having inherited great skill and knowledge
> Your poetry, calligraphy and painting are well
> loved:
> Not attracted by rank and popularity,
> You always despised bowing bureaucrats.

Although written for my teacher, the piece may well be a fitting description of myself.

1916: I was fifty-four.

My teacher Wang Hsiang Ch'i died at the age of eight-five. I went to pay respect to his memory and wept.

In the same year, something very annoying happened. I had developed a special love for Sung poetry and although I hated to imitate, I sometimes did compose lines that sounded rather like the poets of Sung. I had written some three hundred poems. Somehow the whole lot was stolen, and I thought it was very bad taste of the thief.

"Remembering Pa Ta Shan Jen"

Chapter 7 Settling in Peking

1917: I was fifty-five.

I had not left Hunan for a long time, but life had
been very unsettled because of the civil war. Local
bandits took advantage of the situation and created
havoc everywhere. I was persuaded by Fan Ts'en
Hsiang to move to Peking where life was more
peaceful and it was possible to make a living by
selling art. So I started my second visit to Peking.

After some moving between Peking and Tientsin,
I put up at Fa Yuan Shrine in Hsi Chuan Hu T'ung.
My scale of fees was promptly displayed at a paper
shop in Liu Li Ch'ang. Chen Shih Ts eng was much
impressed by my seal-engravings and he came to see
me. This proved to be the beginning of a life-long
friendship. Chen was an eminent painter of flowers
and his reputation was great. I wanted him to assess

The Seal: "Wife of Pai Shih."

my *Chieh Shan T'u Chuan* and he said that my conceptions were lofty but my paintings lacked a sense of sublimity. He encouraged me to beat a new path for myself, to have a style of my own and not to curry favour with the common people. This suited me well.

Fan Ts'en Hsiang had a high opinion of my poetry and he wrote an introduction for my *Chieh Shan Yin Kuan Shih Ts'ao* which was published ten years later.

Besides knowing I Shih Fu and Chen Shih Ts'eng in Peking, I also made the acquaintance of Ling Wen Yuan, Lo Tun Yung, Lo Tun Nuan, Wang Chi Lin, Wang Yun, Hsiao Fang Chun, Chen Nien, Yao Hua, Chang Po Chen, and two monks named Tao Chieh and Jui Kuang. I was not too lonely.

I returned to Hunan towards the end of the year.

1918: I was fifty-six. Robbery and kidnapping went rampant. Although I was by no means rich, I was comparatively well off and it was rumoured that I was considered qualified to be kidnapped. When I got wind of this, I with my family took refuge in Tzu Ching Hill, where one of our relatives lived. It dawned on me for the first time that although I loved my home village I might have to get away and live in Peking where it was comparatively peaceful.

1919: I was fifty-seven. I had decided to settle down in Peking. My father was by now eighty-one and my mother seventy-five. They somehow had the premonition that this trip was going to be a different one and that they would seldom be able to see me. Ch'un Chun was reluctant to leave the little property she possessed and preferred to stay

The seal: "Aftermath of 1971"

56

at home with the children, saying that since she was a woman there was no harm to stay behind and that when I got settled down she could then travel between Peking and Hsiang T'an. She also wanted me to find someone to take care of me abroad, a Fu Shih or sub-wife. I was indeed grateful to her for such considerateness. She always thought about my well-being before hers.

It was Spring and pear-flowers were blossoming. It was drizzling and the flowers looked as if in tears. Those were the circumstances in which I left home.

I stayed in the same Fa Yuan Shrine when I arrived in Peking. Prices were not too high then and I was able to make ends meet by engaging in the same trade as before. I was quite homesick and often sleepless at night. I consoled myself by writing short poems. Around the moon festival in the eighth month, I received a letter from Ch'un Chun announcing her plan to come. So I rented some rooms next to the Dragon-Spring Shrine. Soon after her arrival, Ch'un Chun engaged a sub-wife for me, called Hu Pao Chu. She was only eighteen and a native of Szechuan.

Having arranged all the things for my comfort and convenience, Ch'un Chun returned home accompanied by me.

1920: I was fifty-eight. I took my third son Liang Kun and first grandson Ping Ling to Peking for their education.

At that time, Chu Ta was my idol and I tried to paint like him. However, no one in Peking appreciated the results except Chen Shih Ts'eng. I charged only two silver dollars for painting a fan, which was only half of what other artists did. But still few people came to me. Chen Shih Ts eng persuaded me to change my style somewhat. I created the "Red-flower-black-leave" type of painting. In painting plum-blossoms, I used to adopt the method of Yang Pu Chih of the Sung Dynasty; but Chen Shih Ts eng had said, "To do fine, delicate drawings of plum-blossoms is a waste of time." So I changed my style again.

When a fan painting of mine was seen by Lin Ch'in Nan, he was enthusiastic. He said, "Wu in the South and Ch'i in the North are equals as artists." This was generous praise in view of the high esteem Wu Ch'ang Shih enjoyed. I must admit though that there is some resemblance between Wu's style and mine.

I got to know Hsu Pei Hung, Ho Lu Chih, Chu Wu Yuan and Li Sung An.

In the same year I met Mei Lan Fang.* Mei was most amiable and courteous and every inch a scholar. He had a nice house and planted many flowers. On our first meeting Mei asked me to paint grass insects. He prepared the ink and paper for me and when I had finished he entertained us by singing part of "The Drunken Imperial Concubine." All of us were greatly impressed. Here I must recall one occasion on which I was particularly grateful to Mei Lan Fang. I attended a party given by a ranking official and as I was rather poorly dressed, no one paid any attention to me. I felt rather put off and regretted having come. When Mei Lan Fang arrived, he showed me great courtesy, to the surprise of all. I painted a picture for him entitled "Presenting Charcoal in Time of Snow."

Note: Mei Lan Fang was a famous female impersonator on the Peking operatic stage.

"Quite unexpectedly laughter seeps through the screen and fence,
And one wonders how this old man can survive in this world.
What is there to boast of in this picture of poor cottages?
Before and behind the huts, there are some nice pine trees."

The Seal: "I dream about looking at fishes in a pond."

牡丹為花之王荔枝為果之王獨不論

白菜為菜之王何如

白石

"The peony is the queen of flowers; the lychee is the prima donna of fruits.
How come the white lettuce is not called the princess of vegetables?"

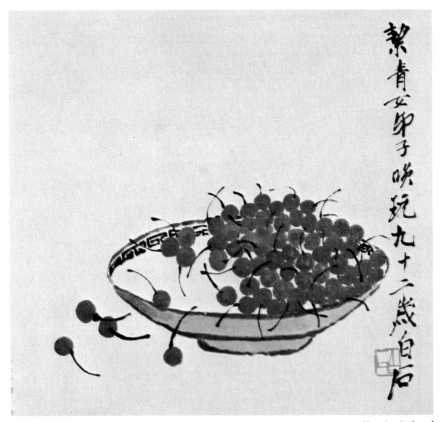

絜青女卯子�玩九十二歲白石

Col. pl. 1

Cherries in bowl

Col. pl. 2

石泉悟画圖

古人粉本非真石
十日工夫畫一泉如
此十年心領暑鳥
君源複未家船

雲派潭

慧沖和
擇沐浴え
吉甲寺
夫澤
寿入昵
知亡

"If one spends 10 days painting a waterfall, in ten years one will understand its mysteries."

Col. pl. 3   **"The picture is dedicated to my foreign friends"**

1921: I was fifty-nine.

I visited Hsiang T'an and was happy to find my parents in good health. The first baby by Pao Chu was born and I called him Liang Ch'ih, it being my fourth son. Ch'un Chun was anxious lest Pao Chu, then only twenty, should be ignorant about child care. She took personal charge of it, slept with it often, having to get up several times a night, even in Winter. She loved the baby very much indeed.

1922: I was sixty.

At the invitation of Chen Shih Ts eng, who was going to Japan with his paintings to attend a Sino-Japanese Art Exhibition, I submitted a number of paintings to be exhibited. It was quite unbelievable, but at the Exhibition all my paintings were sold and at very high prices. Besides, some of my paintings were selected to be exhibited in Paris. After this, my paintings were sought after by many foreigners and my business was booming. I was very much indebted to Chen Shih Tseng for all this.

My grandson died, aged seventeen. He was a good boy. I remember, when we were back in Hsiang T'an, he used to help me plant pear trees round our house, following me about with knife and chisel. His death was a great blow to me. In his memory I wrote these lines:

 If the pear-flowers have feelings,
They should remember him
Who helped to plant them.

The Seal: A finger-print of Chi Pai Shih engraved by himself.

1923: I was sixty-one.

I began to keep a diary, which I called "Three-Hundred-Stone-Seals Studio Memoirs." I was not a good diary man and I often neglected to write anything for days on end. Chen Shih Ts'eng died in Nanking after attending his step-mother's funeral in Dairen, aged forty-eight. I benefited greatly by Chen's advice, which I often accepted. He, on the other hand, was very open-minded. Two lines I wrote testify to our great friendship:

Without me you will not advance
Without you I shall retrograde.

My second son by Pao Chu was born named Ling I.

1924: I was sixty-two.

My son Liang Kun had been learning painting with me for some years and now he had also set himself up as an artist. In fact he could support himself with his own income. His wife Chang Tzu Huan can paint plum-blossoms and they were not bad too.

At a party I gave in honour of Pin K'ai Nan, a native of Hsiang T'an, who was very interested in Buddhism, someone among the guests said, "Now that you are so well-known abroad, why don't you take a trip to Japan where you can make good money with your seals and paintings?" I said, "I have lived here in Peking for the past nine years. I believe in contentment. I am quite happy with what little money I make; why should I have more money. It can only prove to be an encumbrance." Pin K'ai Nan smiled and said, "Judging from what

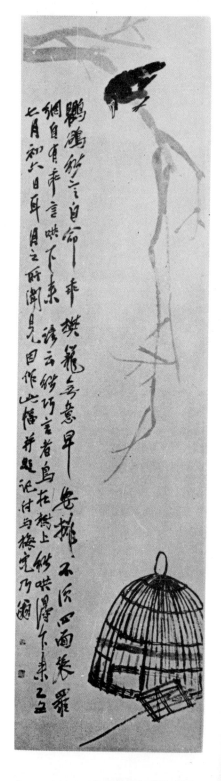

"The mynah boasts of being able to speak;
The cage is prearranged there unsuspected.
There is no need to spread the net all round;
Some eloquent one will soon coax him to come down."

The Seal: "Yearning to hold a fishing rod like in my young days."

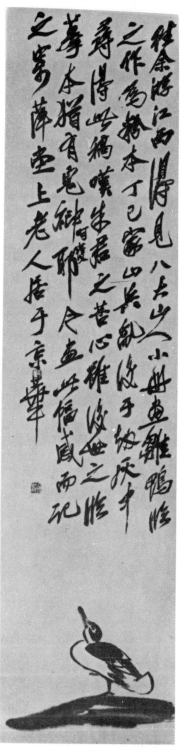

"In bygone days when I visited Kiangsi I saw an album with a picture of a young duck by Chu Ta and I made a copy of it as a model. This was salvaged from the ravages of the civil war. I had remarked how strange it was that the spirits should have helped to preserve it although only a copy. I painted this in order to make a record of my discovery."

The Seal: "Richman with three hundred stone seals."

"One of Chu Ta's albums has a picture of a man scratching his back. This is a copy."

Upper left: a stone rubbing of an arhat

余数岁学画人物三十岁後学
画山水四十岁後專畫花卉虫鸟
近冷厂先生一日携常秀画雪
景余為此水陆绕二十餘年矣此
然蓝元先生壬子印雖醜醜不
得已光绪又酉十月齐璜記不

"I started to draw figures when only a few years old; after thirty, landscape. After forty, I specialised in flowers, grass, insects and birds. Mr. Lan Ann asks for a snow scene, but I have stopped doing landscapes for over twenty years. How can I do it again? But I cannot refuse him and so here it is. I have to go through with it however unsightly the result might be."

see page 13

"The crab is the only creature that can walk sideways. Although one admits that heaven loves life, one cannot but observe that it is also too mischievous in creating the crab."

The seal: "Those who have feelings are prone to be sad"

you say, you can begin to learn Buddhism." With that Pin expounded some Zen principles for my benefit. In 1925, for two months I was seriously ill. Mei Lan Fang started to learn painting grass-insects with me. A fine student, he soon became quite an adept.

1926: I was sixty-four. In Spring, I was on my way to see my parents when I received news in Ch'ang Sha that the road to Hsiang T'an was blocked by fighting. So I had to return to Peking. Soon my son Liang Yuan wrote to say my mother was seriously ill. I was overcome with anxiety but as the civil war was raging fiercely, I could do nothing except to send some money home. The next thing I heard was that my mother had died, aged eighty-two. Before she expired, she had repeatedly asked, "Has Shun Chih come back? I can't wait any more. I have not seen Shun Chih and I can't help thinking of him even after death." I was blinded with tears. I could never get over the fact that I was not beside her bed when she died. Was that the way a son should behave? I was impious in the extreme.

One misfortune followed another. I knew my father was not well, and when a letter came from Liang Yuan in the eighth month, tears streamed down my face before I opened it. I knew it would contain bad news and just as I had expected the letter told of my father's death. I felt a sort of buzzing in my ears and I nearly fainted. Two great losses in one year! It was too much to bear. On the one hand, I was overcome with grief; on the other, I could not help being extremely ashamed of my being so negligent in my duties as son.

1927: I was sixty-five.

I was invited by Lin Feng Mien, principal of the National Art Academy, to teach Chinese painting there. I was very diffident at first but after much persuasion on the part of Lin and friends, I finally accepted. I am glad to say that my experience there was very pleasant and satisfying.

1928: I was sixty-six.

A baby girl was born to Pao Chu. I called her Liang Huan.

1930: I was sixty-eight.

Fan Ts'en Hsiang died. I lost another friend who could talk about poetry with me. My second daughter by Pao Chu was born and I called her Liang Chih.

I had many occasions to visit Chang Garden. Although it was situated in the city, it has all the rural charms. It has many clear streams where one could count the fishes, the water being so clear. Chang Po Ch'en used to invite me to stay there for days and his vivacious sons were often my companions, watching grass-insects and shrimps. Here I painted one of my best pictures of shrimps. I also painted "Spring in Chang Garden."

1932: I was seventy. My favourite pupil Shui Kuang, a monk, died at the age of fifty-five. His death gave rise to many sad thoughts. I had always wanted to give up working, now that I am quite well off for an artist. Why should I carry on struggling. I had written a poem on my state of mind then:

The seal: "Famished old man"

71

I have witnessed the passing away of many friends—
Which of them has taken a single coin with him?
I laugh and warn myself saying, "Now that you are
  seventy,

You should take a rest having toiled for so long!"

Alas, this was not to be, much as I would wish.
I suppose I shall have to work till I die.

Since the fall of Shenyang to Japanese hands,
all who could afford it went South for refuge. My
paintings were much sought after by the Japanese
but I tried all sorts of ways to avoid painting for
their benefit.

Although I usually paint things of everyday life,
I did not aim at verisimilitude. I believe that
only when a painting becomes lifelike without
contrivance can it reach sublimity. I had written
something on this:

Painting life I do not strive for mere likeness;
I do not mind lowering my reputation thereby.

Naturally my pictures are not appreciated by the
common crowd. I have explained this in the lines:

I own two hands with surpassing skill,
But it is difficult to scratch where it itches.

I am always against being tied down by artistic
tenets of various schools:

I always hold in contempt underlings of the great;
I am ashamed to boast about partisan virtues.

I detest imitation of old masters. I have said
this:

72

Beyond the hills, terraces and mansions;
Beyond the clouds, tall peaks—
Artists for a thousand years
Have been composing pictures this way.

Only Chen Shih Ts eng, the monk Shui Kuang
and Hsu Pei Hung went along with me. When I did
landscapes, I took great pains to compose so that it
did not fall into the trap of the old masters. It was
not a coincidence that I very seldom painted landscapes after fifty, when I had begun to believe I
had little time to spare. From that time onwards I
had omitted landscape painting in my scale of fees.
The few landscapes I painted, namely "Lecturing
by a Lily Pond," "Wan Li Lou Landscape," "Lamp-
light in the Rain," "Liao Tung Yin Kuan Poetry
Discussion" and "Wo Lan I Tz'u" have each certain
special qualities.

1933: I was seventy-one.

On the twenty-third of the twelfth month, I com-
memorated the one hundred and twentieth anni-
versary of my grandmother's birth. I made this a
special occasion because I felt I owed her too much
to pass it unmarked. I engaged some Buddhist
priests to say prayers for her spirit. I wrote the
following on a piece of paper and put it together
with the paper-money and other things and burnt
them as an offering to her: "To Grandmother Ch'i,
n'ee Ma, aged one hundred and twenty this year,
for her benefit in the Nether-world. Other spirits
please stay away:

I, your eldest grandson, am now seventy-one.
Taking refuge from bandits, I am living in Peking,

"I have seen Chu Ta's painting of a bird on a branch; it was a wild bird. Now this drawing of mine is of a domestic bird, but not any less interesting."

The Seal: "I fear the green hills will laugh at my not being my former self."

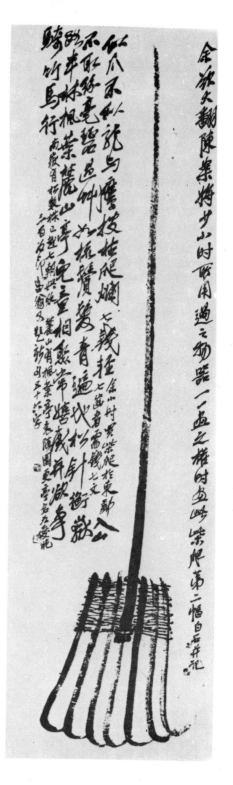

"I want to refresh my memory and paint all the implements I had used when a child. This is a bamboo rake. It looks like a cucumber, not dragon or horse; it costs seven coins and it is used for raking dry leaves. It does not take away anything that is still green. It combs through grass like going through black hair.

The road to the Heng Mountains is full of pine needles. Beneath the Lushan pavilion, there is a lot of maple leaves. When children get together they like to play bamboo horses with the rake."

The stal: "Grasses and plants are not
        necessarily without feelings"

unable to return to my native village. Though nearing death, I cannot go and sweep my grandmother's grave. This is heart-rending."

1934: I was seventy-two.

I used to possess some three hundred stone seals and I had called my study "The Three-hundred-seals Studio." These were taken away from me by looters during years of civil strife. In Peking, I collected again some three hundred seals and the name of my studio was once more meaningful.

The way I engrave a seal is like the way I write which is I never go back on a single stroke once it is on paper. Similarly once the knife has struck, it never goes back. My knife only goes two directions, latitudinal and longitudinal—unlike others who allow their knives to go in all directions, back and forth. Those who are discerning will understand why I engrave the way I do. I do not make tracings on the stone in the process. I went according to the direction and rhythm of the characters. The way most people treat their stones can only be called scraping and scratching. I always say, "Things should be done promptly and to one's own complete satisfaction—the more so in the case of seal engraving, which, being something to be enjoyed, should be pursued without any feeling of encumbrance . Otherwise it cannot be done well."

Another son by Pao Chu was born and given the name Liang Nien.

1935: I was seventy-three.

The year saw many signs of my deterioration.

Pain spread from my right arm down to my leg and what worried me more were the frequent spells of dizziness.

The seal: "1935"

76

"This is a draft of a painting I did for Kuo-wu in Yinchou."

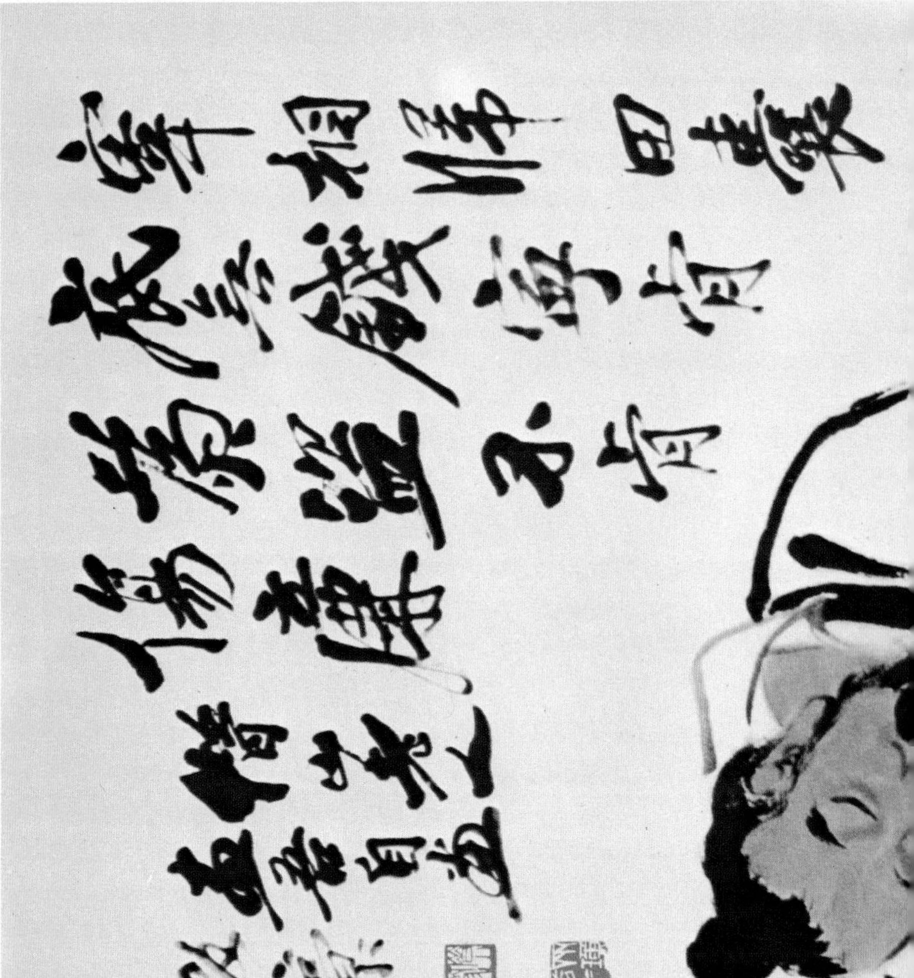

Col. pl. 5

"The prime-minister has retired to his native village penniless, but he would rather be a thief than a corrupt official"

Squirrels and Cherries reproduced from a woodblock print.

For poem see page 142
The seal: "I make few acquaintances —
to avoid gossip and scandal"

"After exhausting all his resources, he succeeds in producing only a single pill of immortality, but the dull-eyed common people still regard him as a famished mendicant."

The seal: "The superior person will be badly spoken of"

I took Pao Chu for a trip to Hsiang T'an. It was twenty years since I last went there. The house was still in good condition and everything was spic and span, thanks to the good management of my sons. Only Ch'un Chun was miserably thin and emaciated. She was seventy-four now. After a stay of some days, I left quietly. I could not bear saying goodbye to Ch'un Chun in her condition.

During the short stay, I swept the grave of my parents. In my diary, I had this entry: "I never had an opportunity to return the love my parents bore me. Now that I want to do so, they are not here to receive it." I engraved a seal bearing the characters "Regretful-Crow Hall" to remind me of the occasion.

I had a bad fall and seriously sprained my ankles. I was almost crippled.

1936: I was seventy-four.

I had always wanted to buy a piece of land to be used later for my burial. So far I had not succeeded. However, Wang Sung Nien at my request had written for me seven characters to be used on the tombstone "Ch'u Shih Ch'i Pai Shih Chih Mu,"— the grave of Ch'i Pai Shih, commoner. I had already got several persons including Ch'en San Yuan, Yang Yun Shih to write epitaphs for me.

A certain Mr. Wang who lived in Szechuan had asked me through a friend to engrave seals for him —we had corresponded several times and became good friends. An express letter from him came one day beseeching me to visit Szechuan. This was followed by a telegram. As Pao Chu was a native of Szechuan, it was natural for her to want me to accept the invitation. So we took our two sons and

The seal: "I was seventy three"

The Seal: "One should emulate the virtuous."

The Seal: "Forever labouring for one's offspring, like horses and oxen."

"Shih Tao at Work"

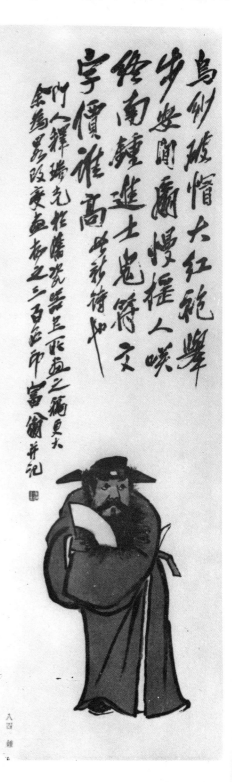

A portrait

went on the journey. After staying in Pao Chu's village home for a few days and having performed the proper rites at her mother's grave we continued our journey, and after a few days found ourselves in Cheng-tu. Here I met Fang Hsu, Chin Sung Ch'en, Ch'en Shih I, Huang Pin Hung.

Central Szechuan was even more beautiful than Kweilin. I visited Ch'ing Ch'eng and O Mei mountains.

Someone asked me on my return to Peking why I did so little in the way of poetry and painting on the trip. Was I unhappy about something? I said, "No, why should I be unhappy. Four of us went there and the same number came back. There is nothing to sadden me. Only Szechuan was always so foggy. That was most annoying particularly as I wanted most to see the mountains." A poem describes this:

Angry billows make a noise like thunder in Spring;
The river fog rises to join the sky and lingers
How I wish that the Red Crow would end all that:
I have come all the way to see the mountains!

The Seal: "An old man, I weep over the death of Fan Shan."

"After a long day how refreshing to have
   a cool and quiet evening
Making friends with seagulls flying over
   the slender willows.
In order that the hills and streams may
   not feel lonely
I linger here fishing though knowing no
   fishes are around."

The Seal: "My family live beneath the
   Heng mountains."

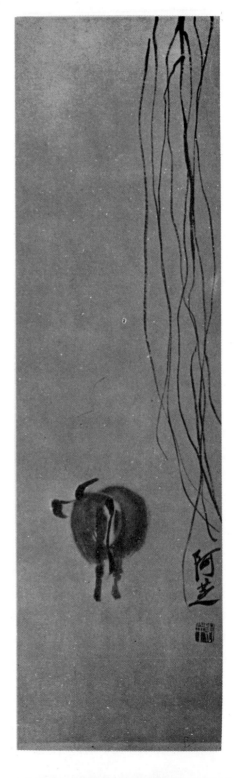

Buffalo and Willow-leaves

The Seal: "I started learning to compose
Tzu poetry at fifty."

Shrimps

Fruit and Wasp

Frogs

Monk with Frog

Dragonflies

The Seal: "The praise of the world is
not worth coveting."

Lychees

Peaches and flowers

Col. pl. 13   **Crane**

Col. pl. 14

Trees & Cottages

Chapter 8 The Recluse

1937: I was seventy-seven.

My real age was seventy-five. The reason why I say my age was seventy-seven was that I was advised by a fortune teller to avoid "seventy-five" because I was supposed to be under evil influence at that age. I was also told to recite the Buddhist Sutra, to wear some charms made of gold and to avoid people born in the years of the dragon, the dog, the ram and the cow.

Peking and Tientsin fell to the Japanese.

1938: I was seventy-eight.

My seventh son (fourth by Pao Chu) was born and I named him Liang Mo. By now Pao Chu was thirty-seven. My grandson Ping Sheng was born, son of my fourth son Liang Ch'ih, who was now eighteen. My sixth son Liang Nien died, aged five.

The Seal: "I paint the way I please."

He was a remarkable child. Even at the age of three, he had already practised self-denial. When something he liked very much was given to him, he would keep part of it for his parents. I was quite disconsolate at the loss. I stopped diary-writing.

1939: I was seventy-nine. Since the fall of Peking I very seldom appeared in public although I had been approached very often for my paintings. In order to avoid people who came to bother me, I put a notice on the main gate saying, "Old man Pai Shih has heart trouble and will not be able to receive guests." I was in fact suffering from a minor heart condition and it was convenient to use this excuse, but since I could not carry on without selling pictures and seals, I added this, "For paintings and seals please contact my agent, the South Paper Store." A lot of people made good money by hoarding and they all wanted my paintings to decorate their homes and so my business throve. At the beginning of the following year, I posted this notice on the gate: "Local and foreign officials who wish to acquire my paintings can negotiate by deputy. They need not come personally. It is not customary for officials to visit commoners because such visits bring ill fortune." I also appended certain conditions of sales like: "No reduction of prices, no invitations to restaurants accepted, no photographs," together with a note in small letters: "I am eighty now. Six silver dollars for one foot square, plus twenty cents per dollar. No personal favour can be considered. All applicants must pay according to the scale of fees." Some time later, I posted this: "Do not make request on behalf of others. No payment to interpreters. I have a heart

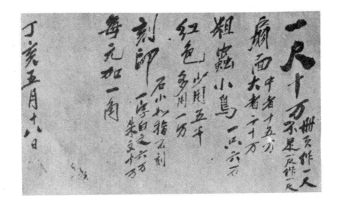

Scale of fees (1947)
- One foot: 100,000 yn. (album leaf considered one foot; under one foot same as one foot.)
- Fans: medium sized, 150,000 yn. large 200,000
- Large insects or small birds: 60,000 each
- Red: sparingly, 5,000; profusely 10,000
- Seal: finger-sized stone not accepted
  White characters: 6,000 each
  Red characters: 10,000 each
- 10 cents per yn. added to fees

The Seal: "The spirit is often an enemy of the body."

"Such diversity of Creation! Nature
Loves life but discriminates not,
Alas, between good and evil.
The myriad shrimps that fill the
    seas & rivers —
How they wish to be changed into
    locusts to greet the skies!"

The seal: "Looking at the white clouds,
        I feel reluctant to leave home"

condition and I cannot cope with too many requests." In the second month of the year, I received news from my eldest son Liang Yuan that Ch'un Chun had died in the first month, aged seventy-nine. She had been in the family since thirteen, never complaining in spite of poverty and privations. Her death was a great blow to me and no words could express my sorrow. I composed this couplet in her memory:

I cannot understand why the matchmaker who
    bound us together should put us asunder;
Let me ask the dark-faced Yama who controls our
    life and death why he bars our reunion.

In Liang Yuan's letter he also mentioned that Ch'un Chun on her death bed repeatedly told my sons and grandchildren to take good care of me and not let me get into a temper.

1941: I was eighty-one. Pao Chu had lived with me for over twenty years. She had been hard working and patient. After the death of Ch'un Chun, my relatives came and persuaded me to install her as my rightful wife. Accordingly, in the fifth month, I invited over twenty relatives and friends in Peking to come as witnesses. There and then I divided up my little property into six parts—three parts to my sons by Ch'un Chun and the other three to my sons by Pao Chu. Immediately after this I performed the ceremony of installing Pao Chu as my wife. Pao Chu was quite happy.

1942: I was eighty-two.

Since I am getting on in age, I have long been meditating as to where I should be buried. I took a

"It was commonly said that if any part of a creature resembles a corresponding part of the dragon, that creature can become a dragon itself. Now the shrimp's head resembles the dragon. Can it become a dragon?"

The seal: "There is nothing that cannot be done; there are things that should not be done" fancy to the Wan An Cemetery on the western suburb and wanted to reserve a space for my own grave, having already got my epitaph written by my old friend Wang Sung Nien, a commemorative note each by Ch'en San Yuan, Wu Pe Chiang, and Yang Yun Shih. But I had procrastinated and never got down to buying a plot . Then I thought about T'ao Jan T'ing which would be a very ideal place, being near to the Hsiang Tomb and the Ying Wu Tomb. People visiting these tombs in future years can also come to look at mine. I at last settled on T'ao Jan Ting. In the first month of the year, I took Pao Chu and my youngest son to visit the place and I was quite happy with the location. However, since all my children and grandchildren were in Hunan, I was afraid lest they should insist on my being buried in our own native village. So, I wrote a letter giving Chang Tz'u Chi the power of attorney to execute my wish as regards my burial place.

1943: I was eighty-three.

It was six years since Japan invaded China. I had hung up a notice: "No order for paintings accepted," the reason being that since I was already over eighty, I did not want to be bothered unnecessarily. A misfortune befell me this year. In the twelve month Pao Chu died, aged forty-two. She married me at the age of eighteen and for over twenty years had been most loyal and attentive. Since she always tended to the paper and ink when I painted, she knew my ways and could distinguish my paintings from imitations. Her relations with Ch'un Chun were always harmonious. It was a great pity that she should go before I did.

"Having supper alone in the deep of night, when the crabs are beginning to get fat."

The Seal: "I look at the world's people with disdain."

祖母閒鈴心

始歡　璜幼時牧牛

身繋一鈴祖母聞

鈴聲遙知不復倚門矣

也曾捥角教牛

還兒孫照樣耕

春雨老對犁

錫汗滿歈

丙子也屬遊蕭司

九十二歲璜

Col. pl. 7

see page 125

Sparrow and Plum Blossom

Col. pl. 8

小魚煮絲瓜
只有農家
能諳此
風味
白石老人

"Little Fishes Cooked with Loofah
  Gourd:
Only farmers can enjoy this wonderful
  dish."

The Seal: "Contentment dispels
    misfortune."

"Can rain or good weather be called forth? I have heard your cries, as if trying to induce rain or good weather. Can a spouse be expelled, you are the only male in the animal world that may be said to do just that."

寄萍老人老年作

Oil Lamp with Cicada

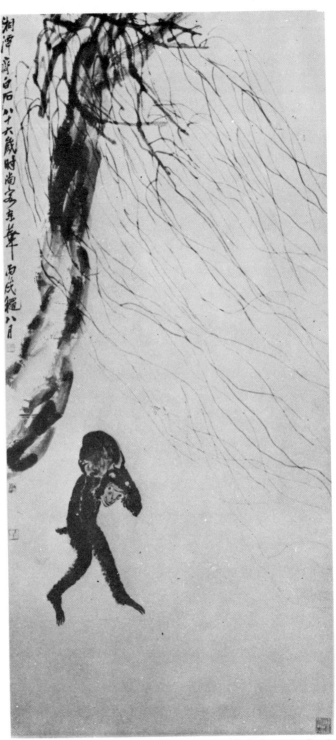

Monkey carrying Peach

1944: I was eighty-four.

I was full of indignation towards the invaders. I had few opportunities to vent my feelings and so when Hu Leng An asked me to inscribe a landscape of his, I wrote this:

Your scroll reminds me of former days
When our great country was unspoiled.
Under the lamp I looked at your picture many
    times,
And lamented the state of our rivers and hills.

I had stopped selling my paintings, but continued to paint every day. I gave all my paintings to my children. I once painted a picture "Fishing-cormorant and Boat" and had this inscription on it:

What beautiful mountains and streams all
    destroyed!
But the cormorant knows nothing except
    the day's meal.
The fisherman cares not the country's rise
    or fall;
Drunken he ties his little boat to a willow
    branch.

When my pupil Li K'u Shan asked me to write something on a picture of his, entitled "The Cormorant," I made this inscription: "This is a fish-eating bird; it does not eat cereal nor its own kind; Sometimes when the river runs dry, some cormorants would die of hunger. The surviving but hungry cormorants would refuse to eat the dead cormorants' flesh when fishermen feed them with it." There is a saying: "The cormorant does not eat cormorant meat." This was meant to be a satire on quislings who prey on their own country people. On a painting of rats I wrote the following:

Grapes and Vine

Rats, how plentiful!
What havoc!
After biting my fruits
They eat my corn.
The candle is waning and the dawn is breaking
And it is late Winter.

On a painting of crabs, I wrote this:

Everywhere in the country are grasses and mud.
How much longer can you go your way?
Last year there were many of you,
This year your number has decreased.

This was a satire on the invaders meaning that their
feet of clay will soon be dragged down the mire.
Some people advised me not to be so outspoken.
My own thinking was since I was already so old, I
can lose little. In the sixth month I suddenly
received a letter from the Art Academy offering
me some coal. Coal was difficult to come by in
those days and this sudden offer came as a surprise.
But realising that the Academy was controlled
indirectly by the invaders, I declined the offer with
the excuse that since I was not a member of the
Academy's staff, it must have made a mistake in
offering me the coal.

At the recommendation of my friends a certain
Miss Hsia Wen Chu took up the job as my nurse.

1945: I was eighty-five.

In the third month I had a dream: Standing in
front of the Borrowed Hill Chamber I saw some
undertakers carrying an open coffin heading directly
towards my house. I thought in my dream that the

coffin must have been intended for me. I was very
unhappy for the rest of day. On the fourteenth of
August, the Japanese unconditionally surrendered.
I was so excited that I was sleepless the whole
night. The clouds and mist dispersing, as it were,
we saw the sky and sun again. Everyone in Peking
rejoiced. Who would have thought that civil strife
would follow so closely. Inflation set in and corrup-
tion was rampant.

1946: I was eighty-six.

I started to sell paintings and seals again. My
fifth son Liang I graduated from the Art School of
Fu Jen University. He was quite competent and
many people said that they could not tell his paintings from mine. At the invitation of the Nanking
authorities I held an exhibition there. After that
I held an exhibition in Shanghai and sold two
hundred odd paintings. The amount of bank notes
I brought back with me was impressive, but owing
to the inflation, it was not enough to buy ten bags
of flour. What a joke! I regretted having taken the
trouble. My daughter Liang Huan died at the age of
nineteen. Ever since the death of her mother she
had been unhappy and this probably was one of
the causes of her own death.

1947: I was eighty-seven.

Many of my friends persuaded me to go and live
in Nanking or Shanghai and someone suggested that
I should go and head the West Lake Art Academy.
I was a disillusioned man. My hopes for a better
China after the Japanese surrendered were shattered.
The national paper currency had become almost
waste paper. A small loaf cost two hundred thou-

sand *yuan* and a dinner out cost ten million. People hoarded up things instead of banknotes and my paintings become one of their objects of hoarding. They came with bundles of banknotes for my paintings and when I looked at the pile of pictures I painted I was a little frightened at the sight. Why should I waste my time and energy in exchange for a lot of useless waste paper which can hardly buy enough to keep me alive? So, with a deep sigh I hung up a sign saying, "No orders accepted temporarily."

The Seal: "Aged 90."

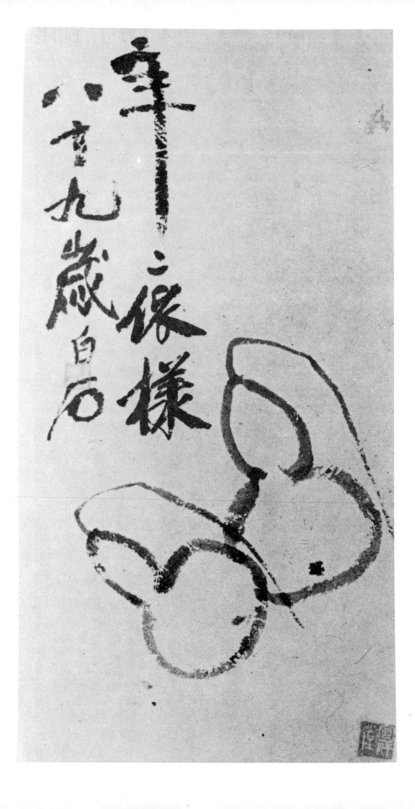

THE PAINTINGS OF CH'I PAI SHIH

An Appreciation

THE PAINTINGS OF CH'I PAI-SHIH

An appreciation
by
Dr. May-ching Kao Yeung

Chinese art from the seventeenth to the nine-teenth century was dominated by the literati painters the "four Wangs", namely Wang Shih-min, Wang Chien, Wang Hui, and Wang Yuan-chi, who advocated an eclectic style based on the great masters of the past. Since then, Chinese artists had been trying to break away from it. They sought inspiration from nature instead of adhering to rigid conventions. Artists who were concerned with the future of Chinese art hoped to revitalize it by introducing Western concepts and techniques, re-sulting in the founding of a "modern" school which vociferously challenged traditional aesthetic values. In the thirties, however, some of the protagonists

The Seal: "I bathe in orchid-water and wash my hair
with the perfume of flowers."

113

of Western art, notably Hsu Pei-Hung, Liu Hai-su, and Lin Feng-mien, disillusioned by Western excesses, fell back on their native tradition to seek new directions. Amidst the turmoil and controversies, one humble artist who started life as a carpenter from Hunan, stood aloof. Using the traditional medium of brush and ink, he sought inspiration from the individualist tradition in Chinese painting but at the same time enriching it with elements of folk art and enlivening it with direct observation of nature. He succeeded in breaking away from the sterile influence of the orthodox school and introducing a new path for contemporary Chinese painting completely independent of Western influence. He was Ch'i Pai-shih.

Born into a poor peasant family, Ch'i Pai-shih was apprenticed to a carpenter at the age of twelve. Progressing from the beginner's rough work, he learned to make fine, delicate objects and to carve decorative furniture. It was while selecting motifs for a design that he discovered the *Chieh-tzu-yuan hua-chuan* (Painting Manual of the Mustard Seed Garden). He copied the pictures over and over again until he had mastered the manual's various techniques. Gradually, he became known not only as an excellent carver of flowers, but also as a painter of figures, flowers and birds in the *kung-pi* style.

Not until he was twenty-seven did Ch'i Pai-shih have the opportunity to study painting and classical literature with a knowledgeable teacher. While still a carpenter he came to know two professional painters, Hsiao Hsian-kai and Wen Shao-K'o, who taught him to paint protraits. Since there was a

114

great demand for family ancestral portraits as well as pictures of legendary gods, Ch'i gave up his carpenter career and became a professional painter. As such, he was quite successful. He worked in a variety of traditional styles, but much of the work executed before the age of forty was undistinguished.

Several things should be noted, however, during this early period. Ch'i Pai-shih was primarily a self-taught artist with a craftsman's background. Hence one could expect him to hold a high respect for technical perfection. His art is deeply rooted in the folk art tradition. His simple direct approach coupled with his use of bright and gay colors inherited from his early years, remained with him throughout his career.

During the year 1902-1920 when he painted the Chieh-shan-t'u-chuan and the Twenty Four Scenes of Shih-meng, his art went through a period of transition brought about by his extensive travels and encounters with scholars and artists. He experienced a dramatic change in his artistic life. In the words of Li K'o-jan, Ch'i Pai-shih "broadened his artistic vision and turned away from mere formal likeness. He graduated from folk art to the classical tradition; a transition from vuglar to refined taste."

During these years of transition, Ch'i was greatly influenced by the seventeenth-century individualists, Shih-t'ao and Pa-ta Shan-jen. An example could be found in a landscape done after the age of forty. In this rather small work, Ch'i Pai-shih seems to be stretching the traditional technique to its limits, and arrives at what appears to be a very daring design of five overlapping hills, each covered with long trailing lotus-leaf veins, which dominates the entire composition. It reminds one of Shih-t'ao, who was known for his bold designs and daring brushwork. Even the little hut precariously placed on top of the mountain and the lone wanderer leisurely strolling beneath the hills are favourite compositional devices of Shih-t'ao.(col. pl. 2)

Ch'i Pai-shih was a great admirer of Pa-ta Shan-jen whose sense of design, expert use of ink, lofty feeling and introspectiveness were sources of inspiration to Ch'i.

Following the advice of a fellow artist Ch'en Heng-k'o,* Ch'i Pai-shih attempted to assimilate influences from the early Ch'ing individualists and to incorporate these influences to his earlier background of folk art. The new style which evolved gradually is characterized by simplicity, vigour, and elegance. It shows a sense of life and humanity, not without humour and satire. He became particularly interested in portraying small living creatures such as grasshoppers, dragonflies, prawns, crabs, frogs, and sparrows. For his flowers, fruits, and vegetables, he used robust reds and yellows against black, often used to emphasize a certain part of the pictures (page 137)

The innovative style that Ch'i matured can be illustrated by a number of examples. "Red Plum Blossoms and Sparrow" (col. pl. 8) is a work painted when Ch'i was around seventy. It shows a lone sparrow standing on top of a rock behind which emerges a branch of red plum blossoms. The composition as well as the loose calligraphic treat-

*Styled Ch'en Shih Tseng

116

Maid-servant of the Cheng family

"Beyond the curved balustrade, laughter can be heard
And a gentle breeze wafts forth a delicate perfume;
I was fond of her and especially remember this:
She said, "I am Cheng Kang-cheng the great scholar.""

Col. pl. 10

"The fish-net having dried,
The wine having been consumed,
I wash my feet
And go to bed
Nor take any heed
Of the evening sun
Outside my door."

ment of the theme is reminiscent of Pa-ta Shan-jen, but Ch'i Pai-shih had added colour to the composition and replaced the cold and hostile birds of Pa-ta by a sparrow whose liveliness is captured with a few strokes of colour wash. The total effect is at once spontaneous and vigorous, giving testimony to the painter's love for life and nature.

Another painting which merits our attention is an album leaf painted about ten years later at the age of eighty. The composition is again very simple, consisting of a gourd and a ladybird (cover). Three broad strokes — and Ch'i has given us a fresh and succulent fruit with a tiny ladybird perching on it! The bright yellow of the gourd and the intense red of the ladybird create a pleasing contrast never attempted by traditional artists. Underlying this work of art are the joy of living and a loving sympathy for the little insects and vegetables that form part of the painter's repertoire.

Ch'i Pai-shih achieved a special reputation as a painter of flowers and birds which became his main preoccupation. However, he continued to paint landscapes and figures, though less frequently, employing free and forceful strokes in refreshingly simple compositions. A good example of his later landscape is found in a work painted when the artist was about seventy-five years old. It depicts a quiet village by the river, the sky tinted by the rays of the setting sun. The main elements in the composition are unconventionally placed at the top, while the river is indicated by some arbitrarily drawn strokes covering two-thirds of the painting. The conception is at once refreshing and novel. The inscription, tells us of the artist's yearning for the simple life of a fisherman who retires after his work is done, even though the sun is only just beginning to set (col. pl. 10).

In technique, Ch'i's landscape paintings show that he had freed himself from the stereotyped forms and conventions of the "Four Wangs" and those handed down from generation to generation by other schools. By expressive content, Ch'i was able to communicate through his little landscapes, whether it be a village by the river, or some black cormorants gathered on a sand bank, (page 80) a feeling of something actually experienced—possibly not a profound experience, but a personal and genuine one.

His figure paintings owe little to traditional models; they are often pregnant with humour and sarcasm. Whether it be an imaginary portrait of the painter Shih-t'ao (page 83) or a drunken official fast asleep (col. pl. 5), his figures are always executed with the utmost simplicity and freshness.

But Ch'i Pai-chih's contribution to contemporary Chinese painting lies not only in bringing the individualist tradition to a new plateau, but also in breaking away from tradition in his choice of subject matter. Paintings belonging to the latter category include "dish of fish and basket of loofah gourds" (page 101); "bird trapped inside a cage" (page 102)'tiny mouse and burning oil lamp"(page 1 43) "procelain container laden with red cherries" (col. pl. 1); "well-used ink stone, brushes, teapot, and spray of orchids" (page 132). Other compositions include abacus (page 165) and "rake" (page 75). Many of these themes were formerly considered by the literati painters unfit for artistic treatment, but here Ch'i handles them in a manner most aesthetically satisfying. These themes, together with his plants and animals—are commonly seen and are closely related to the ordinary daily life of the people. The pictures become Ch'i's personal statements on the world around him.

We find in Ch'i's art simple and sparse forms, yet we are able to perceive a high sense of reality which enlivens all his pictures. Perhaps the artist himself could explain it best. He once said, "The excellence of a painting lies in its being alike, yet unlike. Too much likeness flatters the vulgar taste; too much unlikeness deceives the world." Likeness can be achieved by objective observation and good craftsmanship, but "unlikeness" further requires imagination and a creative instinct. Poised between realism and idealism, Ch'i Pai-shih has left us many great works that capture both the outer form and the inner spirit of the natural world.

Ch'i Pai-shih's mature style was achieved by the fusing of the individualist and the folk art tradition and a keen observation of nature. We have seen the influence of Shih-t'ao and Pa-ta on his artistic development; and he has shown great admiration for the Yang-chou individualists of the eighteenth century. As for contemporary artists, he was closest to Wu Ch'ang-shih , for whom he had great respect and affection. His style in the free calligraphic manner could be considered a continuation of the tradition of Chao Chih-ch'ien and Wu Ch'ang-shih and could ultimately be traced to the Ming painter Hsu Wei and the seventeenth and eighteenth century individualists. In spite of the fact that he received only a modicum of the kind of scholarly education which was considered essential to a painter, he was more than a worthy successor to this lineage. By sheer genius and sustained industry, he has established this school as the mainstream of contemporary Chinese painting.

"You make people think of wine but you are heartless wretches"

MORE POEMS

予少貧為牧童及
木工一飽無時而酷好
文藝為之八十餘年
今將百歲矣吳作畫
凡數千幅詩數千首
治印亦千餘國內
外竟言齊白石畫
予不知其究何所
取也卯与詩則知
之者稍希予不知
知之者之為真知否
不知者之有可知者

否將以問之天下後
世然老且無力吾兒
良已裹卲老人
自喜之作罕示
人者友人黎劭西
先生並為審訂
以待象評予之技
止此予之願亦止此
世欲真知齊白石
者其在斯其在斯
清事斯
齊璜白石

"I was poor when young, being first a cowherd-boy and then carpenter. I often went to work without a decent meal. I was extremely fond of literature and the arts. I must have spent more than eighty of my nearly one hundred years engaged in those pursuits — resulting in several thousand paintings and poems as well as over a thousand seals. My paintings are highly regarded at home and abroad. I wonder what they see in them. Comparatively few know my poems and seals. I am not sure if those who claim to know them really know anything; on the other hand, I wonder if those who confess ignorance did not in fact know part of the truth. This must await the judgment of the world and posterity.

I am old and ineffectual; my son Liang I has collected, and in consultation with Mr. Li Shao-si, printed some of the works that please me but seldom shown to others.

Here is where my skill ends. This is all that I can hope for. Those who want to know the truth about Ch'i Pai Shih — maybe it is here! Maybe it is here! Look for me here! Ch'i Huang Pai Shih."

When can I find the time for poetry?
Perhaps when travelling or else in bed.
The poems I wrote in the last score years,
Of three thousand Mr. Fan has chosen these.

Why strain to polish these woodman-songs!
Our poets of old spurn not everyday speech.
In this our purloined, down-trodden life
The words "many sorrows" are poetry enough.

Ungifted, writing poems is quite an agony.
When a line comes I quickly write it down.
Who cares what fame or shame the poems may bring!
Soon I must lie beneath the grassy mound.

Inscribe on a Picture of a Boy Leading a Buffalo

My grandmother would only feel glad
When she heard the sound of the bell
Which heralded my safe return
From cowherding while a child
With two tufts of hair on my head.

Now my sons and grandsons
Are out farming in the spring rain;
But I being old and feeble
Can only stare at the hoe and plough
Suffused with shame and regret.

Inscription on a Picture of Narcissus and Stone of Grotesque Shape

The stone is grotesque like a monkey,
The narcissus is unfeeling like ice.
The artist has the heart of a monk
Having broken the world's chains.

Setting Fire to My Poems

I have burnt all my poems, you know,
How can a starving worm produce silk?
I love writing poems but my vocabulary is small;
After so much trouble, why be a laughing stock?

Reminiscences

When I was young I loved to roam abroad
Casting not a backward glance at my home village.
The forest was all peaceful; not a bird stirred.
And I had an abundance of good paper for my art.
Now that I am growing old, I loath all affairs
Though one cannot avoid family worries in time of war.
Who sympathizes with me? Only the lotus flowers
Which wither in the cold rain beside the little house.

Meeting Mei Lan Fang

I remember when in the good old days
A poor man may be respected by dukes and princes.
Here in the City of Swallows none knows me
Save Master Mei who greets me by name.

Picking up a Piece of Bamboo
I used it as a Fishing Rod

I want very much to fish beside the little pond,
Having tired myself with reading the old tomes.
The rod must not be over five feet long
Lest its shadow frighten the mandarin ducks.

Plum-Blossoms

It was the year before last when I saw a sea of flowers
Diffusing its perfume under a cold bleak sky.
The old man of the village saw this too with me,
And meeting now we look at each other in sadness.

O! I should have taken refuge in the West Lake.
When my family told me there was no more rice
I smiled and took my desk out in the open
And painted the poet Lin Fu beneath the plum-blossoms.

Seeing a Child go to School

Everywhere there are children;
Every morning they want to play.
Why should the old man here
Alone take you to school?

There is nothing wrong with learning,
And you'll come back to mother soon.
Take care lest the stream of tears
Drip through your bright red coat.

The seal: "In previous life,
a gong-hitting monk"

Ink-stone

When you are smooth and moist I am happy;
If you are broken I shall starve;
When you are intractable, I sigh.

Pen-Brush

I have painted and written so much
My broken brushes have heaped up like a tomb.
But what good does it do to the world?
O my brush! My brush!
I should be glad to share your fate.

Laughing at Myself

What's the use of official rank?
I have my art and that is enough.
Engraving till late I forget to sleep;
I practise calligraphy instead of attending Court.
My teeth may be loose but I draw no stipend;
I live on my own labour not on the people.
I am not blind and my hands are still supple;
I laugh at myself for being such an old freak.

I Saw This

For idleness I cannot compare with some people —
From morning till night I wield my writing brush.
How I admire the leisurely monk with naught to do
Save feeding chickens beneath the grape vines.

Picture of a Flowing Vine
Acquired by an American

With one sweep of the brush, a hundred feet of hanging vine!
So dense its leavage, the sun hardly shines through.
When you hang it high up your parlour wall
Its purple-snow perfume will fill the morning air.

Inscribed on a Picture of a Vine

The paddy field is rich with water of the Hsiang
But after the ravages of war it is quite worthless.
Who would come to buy my paintings at such a time?
A hundred-foot vine hangs unseen in the afternoon mist.

The seal: "Half deaf"

Toy-Tumbler
(A Satire on Bureaucrats)

(1)

A plaything for children, it is a clever device —
Fallen it leaps up again without any help.
It wears a dark cap on a level with the brow;
Though it has no heart nor guts, it has rank.

(2)

Grey robe and white fan — he looks like a mandarin;
He does not fall, a tumbler made of clay.
Should he perchance be broken into pieces
Could one find there any guts or heart?

(3)

I once visited a temple on the Southern Mountain
And spent three coins to buy this earthen tumbler.
I don't complain about what I pay for rice and firewood
Because I sell pictures of tumblers at good prices!

Remembering Old Home at Star Pond

The blue sky issues forth a Spring breeze
Which in no time bleaches our hair white.
The melon and mulberry fields are same as before
But there is none, alas, to call me child.

Planting Vegetables

With our own hands we feed ourselves till old;
I having tilled the soil, my wife puts in the sprouts.
If I have no meat, I am not a bit worried
So long as my yards are green with vegetables.

The Seal: "The mountain flowers in my home village are blossoming now."

Thinking of Lychees

I can no more visit the South again,
With drooping trees heavy with red lychees
Redder than the crest of the crane!
For this I would brave
The hardships of the journey
And wish the wind would waft me there —
To Yin Chow.

Inscribed on a Picture of Withered Lotus

A middle-aged woman walked beside a lotus pond
With up-tied hair she secretly sighs.
She ponders long and looks at the water:
This is no place for her to comb her hair.
Yesterday the lotus leaves were green
Today the lotus leaves are yellow.
When green it can hardly serve as a mirror;
When yellow all brightness disappears.

Inscribed on a Picture of a Man Looking at Hills

The Autumn wind fans my wine-warm face
As puffed sails one by one pass my boat.
I told the boatman not to be in a hurry
As I want slowly to admire the mountains.

Random Thought

In middle age I call myself Old Master Ch'i.
My mirror says my whiskers are not yet grey.
My paintings bring in enough to feed my children;
My straw hut is spacious enough for a studio.

Landscape

Oh, beautèous pines and refreshing wind!
All this, and the hills and streams
I gather in one vast embrace.
The spirits did it — not my own skill.
Who will remember me after I am gone?

The Tree of Jade

Heartless, only too heartless, the tree of jade!
In one frosty night it sheds all its leaves.
Leaving the poor cicada, shelterless, to moan
And chant with me in the cold bleak wind.

Thinking of Childhood Days

Fiery, fiery the peach-blossom;
Green, green the garden grass.
They recall my happy bell-wearing days.
With a book hung on the buffalo's horn
I fell asleep on its back.
Even the garrulous parrot
Was too slothful to wake me up.

Embarrassed at the High Prices My Paintings Fetched

I once used rouge to colour apricot flowers,
And people were amazed
How every foot of my paintings
Fetched a hundred pieces of gold.
I have always been shy
When my name is mentioned,
But now people in land and sea
Know about old painter Ch'i.

A Breath of Fragrance

Fine flowers blossom here
This mound of grass
On White Stone Hill
In yester years.

Last night their souls returned.
Reclining on my couch
A perfume steals in
And settles on my pillow.

Strolling Beside a Pond

When a breeze blows the willows in the garden dance;
When the pond is calm the fishes can be counted.
This is enjoyment enough for the middle-aged,
And I can linger here musing till dusk.

Little Fishes in a Pond

The stones are moist with the morning rain;
When leisure reigns things are not perturbed.
The fishes in the pond seem to understand —
They come to the surface and listen to my lute.

Looking at Fishes

Before the year of Ting Yi I was lazy as mud,
And never ventured out beyond West Borrowed Hill.
I watched the fishes nipple at peach-blossom shadows
While the Spring breeze tugged gently at my sleeves.

Drawing Crows

The tall pines are not alone in being nostalgic about the
old hill
I can also hear the sounds of spring waters in Star Pond
My concubine has prepared for me ink black as lacquer
But when I start to draw some crows I feel so ashamed
of myself

(Note: The crow is a symbol of filial piety. It is supposed to feed
its parents when they are too old to go out for good.)

The Seal: "Regretful-Crow Hall."

see page 144

The seal: "I would rather be
let down by others"

A Mouse Toppling over an Oil Lamp

Last night I lighted the oil-lamp early
Took off my clothes and went to bed.
A poor family, we only have a coin's worth of oil —
How can it satisfy the mouse's hunger?
O! When can I get a little kitten:
The oil dries up before the sun comes out.

Masters of Painting

Hsu-Wei and Chu-Ta are far above the common herd;
Wu in old age burgeoned with genius.
I do not mind to be a running dog in limbo
And be reborn under their studio roofs.

The Seal: "Possessing heaven's skill."

A Mendicant

People will take pity on you when you are hungry.
What's the use of having money in your own purse?
Leftover rice and soup will fill your stomach enough:
The little dog beside you is happy as a fairy.

Releasing Shu Hua

Shu Hua, a native of Szechuan, was presented to me by Mr. Wang Ch'ih Chun, to grind ink for me. Before she had been with me for a year, my daughter being favourably impressed with her demure and modest manners, begged of me to give her to her son in marriage. I granted her wish. Shu Hua wanted no dowry but hoped to have one of my paintings. So I painted a parrot with this inscription:

Though the hills over the Hsiang River are blue indeed,
I tell my talking parrot not to think too much of home:
Beyond the Peace Bridge underneath the ash tree
I open the cage myself and it breaks my heart.

Siesta in Summer

Taking a siesta within closed doors, how delightful!
More so when one getting on in age has shunned society.
A draught of cool breeze tells me rain has come;
A puff of perfume says the lotuses are blossoming.

Love of Sleep

I lament the world's affairs have stifled life;
Only when old do I know the sweetness of sleep.
Being literate as robbed me of life's real joy;
Writing verses spoils my reputation for being lazy.
I lie on a couch of bamboo in heat and rain;
In Spring's coolness I sun myself in the afternoon.
I laugh at erstwhile companions at fishing
For wasting the evening glory of rivers and lakes.

Inscribed on a Picture of Mother and Baby

In old age one should be like a little babe:
When full it stops crying and has no cares,
Nor frightened by the spring thunder under the eaves.
When it seems to be awake, it's asleep.

Mice

Who would not be jealous about others' affluence?
But you alone wish people to have plenty.
The lattice in my garden is full of grapes —
Sweet or sour, let us share them all.

Three Types of Overplus: The character "Yu" is
used as a pun, meaning "fish" and "overplus"

Lychees

I have no official post and can afford to roam —
For one worldly purpose I have come to Canton.
I eat lychees everyday and receive no visitors —
A commoner, I am harder to find than dukes and counts.

Inscribed on A Self-Portrait of Miss Shan Tao

I was like you twenty years ago;
Now twenty years later you too are old.
Why be so concerned about your own visage?
The coming year will be even less kind than this!

Three Types of Overplus

A painting is the left-over of work;
A poem is a by-product of sleep;
Longevity is an oversight of Calamity.

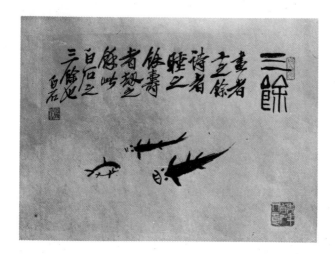

Little Mice Stealing Oil

My oil lamp is dim enough to make one sad
But you will come night after night to steal oil.
I can't write my new poems in the dark.
My paintings don't fetch enough for the oil you need.

The Little Pond

The pond before my house is blue and clear,
But I have no wish to use the hook and line.
The little fishes seem to know my mind,
And placidly swim as if none is about.

The Seal: "My life has always been hard."

Memories of Ch'i Pai Shih

The following accounts are based on personal recollections of Mr. Chang Li Chi, Mr. P. J. Hsu and Mr. Chang Tung who are now residing in Hong Kong.

"When I see an insect, a flower, or a blade of grass, I want it to be full of life. How can I bear to see such goodness and beauty destroyed."

I

When Mr. Hsu Po Jao arrived at Ch'i Pai Shih's little house in the western sector of Peking, a place called Shui Ch'e Hu T'ung, he was intercepted at the door by someone he recognised as an old retired eunuch, a survivor of the Imperial Household. The latter was quick to ask what Mr. Hsu's business was and, upon being told that the purpose of his visit was to buy paintings, he promptly let Mr. Hsu in. Ch'i Pai Shih, now over 90 years old, was in the care of a nurse named Miss Hsia. Mr. Hsu bought some ten paintings at rather reasonable prices and was told if he would go again the following day, he would be shown more. So Mr. Hsu went again the following day. Ch'i Pai Shih was having lunch. He had only one dish—shredded meat with Chinese green. It was a rather frugal lunch, something not expected of a highly successful artist. However,

The Seal: "The flowers are not yet all blossoming and the moon is not yet full."

153

although Ch'i Pai Shih used to have some considerable savings in gold bars, during the Japanese occupation he had to change all into military yen, which became worthless after their defeat. His finances further deteriorated during the days of inflation. Mr. Hsu bought twenty more paintings and when he told the artist that he was the son of Hsu Shen Yu, curator of the Shanghai Metropolitan Museum, Ch'i Pai Shih said he had great respect for the latter. It was through his friend Ch'en Shih Tseng that he had occasions to dine with Hsu Shen Yu. Ch'i Pai Shih offered Mr. Hsu a gift of a painting and asked what subject he preferred. The result was a painting of red leaves and peaches. In this painting, Ch'i Pai Shih personally did the insects, the drawing of which he usually left to his sons. In this painting Mr. Hsu was addressed as Po jao, without the usual designations such as "elder brother," or "Mr.", and so on. This was unusual, but Ch'i Pai Shih said that in these modern times, such designations were quite out of place.

The Seal: "My paintings are all over the world but
the majority of them are fakes."

154

Mr. Chang Tung, journalist, was at one time closely connected with Ch'i Pai Shih and helped to sell many of his paintings. In his opinion, Ch'i was at his best painting half-faded waterlilies.

Mr. Chang recalled how on his first visit Ch'i answered the door (or to be more exact, the inner gate) carrying a large bunch of keys. Apparently Ch'i was rather particular about opening the gate himself, a gate, as it were, to his inner sanctuary. One had to pass two outer doorways before one got there. A retired eunuch kept watch at the front door. He once asked Mr. Chang if he wanted to buy some of Ch'i's paintings from him, upon which Mr. Chang avoided a direct answer, but said that he was sure the discerning doorman would have some very good pieces. It was obvious to Mr. Chang what the doorman offered were probably spurious ones, done by Ch'i's son or some of his students. The doorman was sensible enough not to pursue the subject further.

On one occasion, Mr. Chang observed to Ch'i Pai Shih that there were five other "Ch'i Pai Shihs" in Peking, one in each of the four directions, south, north, east and west; and the fifth was deaf. They were all imitators and they charged the same fees as Ch'i did, which at that time was four silver dollars per piece of about one foot square. Our artist good-humouredly said, "Let that be. People will find it difficult indeed to secure a genuine painting by me. Those who get as far as my front door do not get a genuine piece and those who get as far as the second door share the same fate. Only those who are admitted into this studio through the little iron gate are the lucky ones."

It was common knowledge that Ch'i's son Liang Ch'ih was an excellent painter and it had been remarked that his skill in painting vines and gourds surpassed his father's. Quite a few of the paintings that bore Ch'i's seals were done by Liang Ch'ih. The seals were put on by Ch'i's nurse.

Ch'i Pai Shih once painted a picture of crabs for Mr. Chang in return for the latter's help and invited him to dinner at the Kwei Yang resturant in Peking. Mr. Chang, however, "surreptitiously" paid the bill. Next morning Ch'i's nurse telephoned Mr. Chang to say that Ch'i was feeling quite upset about it and wanted to invite Mr. Chang again to dinner the following night together with all the other guests. Mr. Chang had to accept the invitation, this time taking care not to repeat the bill-paying performance.

Mr. Chang once asked Ch'i Pai Shih how he managed to paint grass insects so exceedingly lifelike. The reply was that he kept them as pets, and gazed at them so often that they became part of his consciousness. It was as if the grass insects would crawl out of his brains, and pass through his pen-brush onto paper! Ch'i was not conversant with theories of art and his teaching at the Central Art Academy at the invitation of Hsu Pei Hung consisted more in demonstration than lecturing.

The seal: "Door-answering octogenarian"

III

Mr. Chang Li Chi moved in the circle of friends of Ch'i Pai Shih, among whom were Pu Hsin Yu and Chen Pan Ting. On one occasion, the last named asked Mr. Chang to take two of his pictures to Shanghai for sale at an exhibition. After selling them Mr. Chang handed the money to one Tsåo Ko Chia, a pupil of Chen's who failed to deliver it to Chen. When Chen reproved Chang behind his back, Ch'i Pai Shih defended the latter vigorously and afterwards wrote a couplet which obliquely des cribed the event:

Chang San sells meat and values friendship;
Liu Sze slanders people without any purpose.

Chang Tao Fan, the then Minister of Education of the Nationalist Government, invited Ch'i Pai Shih to Nanking for the express purpose of giving him tuition in painting. At a dinner reception in which Pu Hsin Yu was present Chang performed the rites installing Ch'i as his teacher. Pu, who was enjoying fame as painter equal to, if not higher than, Ch'i Pai Shih's felt offended and left the party. However, Ch'i did not think the less of Pu because the latter, to him, had one important redeeming virtue: he was very pious towards his mother. Their personalities were quite different. Ch'i neither drank nor smoked, but Pu was a heavy smoker and drinker. Neither of them read newspapers. They were totally unconcerned about the world. Both were noted for their childlike nature.

Ch'i Pai Shih wore two pairs of spectacles when he engraved.

His nurse Miss Hsia followed him everywhere and he jealously watched her movements.

The Seal: "Chang"

ANECDOTES

There is nothing like drinking

I

*From Hsieh Hui Shan's article "Speaking of Ch'i Pai Shih" (*Ta Jen vol. 29) :*

When I first met Ch'i Pai Shih, he was already 86. Ch'i answered the door and took out a bunch of keys from his waist pocket. It must have weighed over half a catty. I understand he was in the habit of being in charge of all the keys in the house, including those for his silver boxes, painting cabinets and rice storage. He was very tall, wearing a mauve-coloured long gown, holding a cane with a dragon head for handle, his silver whiskers waving in the wind. He looked more like someone from another

The Seal: "Unworldly moron."

world. He told me he could still eat two bowls of rice and that he had the habit of painting in the morning. He sighed, saying, "I am getting old; when I was your age, I could paint scores of pictures in one morning without being tired."

When Lin Ch'in Nan saw some of Ch'i's paintings, he exclaimed, "This is the greatest painter in north China." He also said that Wu of the South and Ch'i of the North were equals.

The shrimps painted by Ch'i Pai Shih before sixty were not sufficiently life-like — not until he had observed for a long period the shrimps which he kept alive in a bowl. After sixty, his shrimps still lacked movement although they were more elaborately drawn. When he reached seventy, a feeling of transparancy was imparted to his shrimps, and they were infused with life.

In 1946, when Ch'i was in Nanking, he had an occasion to see horse-racing. He stayed for a long time. His personal nurse had persuaded him to go home and take an afternoon nap but Ch'i would not budge, his eyes glued to a galloping horse. He was heard saying, "How can women understand. I have loved horses all my life and one of my regrets is that I had few opportunities to watch horses, much less to draw them."

Ch'i had acquired an interest in seal-engraving when he was thirty-two. On one occasion he met Li Ch'ing An, a noted engraver. When Ch'i begged Li to teach him the art, the latter said, "Carpenter Chih, if you drink up the liquid waste from my water-pipe, I will give you lessons in seal engraving." Ch'i accepted the challenge without hesitation.

"The sound of frogs from the mountain
stream reaches ten *li*."
see page 164

The seal: "Why want an empty name?"

*From Yeh Chien Yu: The Art of Ch'i Pai Shih
(Studies on Ch'i Pai Shih)*

When Ch'i was 91, the author Lao She wanted
him to paint a picture describing a line of poetry,
namely: "The sound of frogs from the mountain
stream reaches ten *li*." This was a tall order, which
took the old man several days to execute. The
result was a four-foot scroll depicting a cascading
stream with a few tadpoles here and there.
The atmosphere of the poetic line has been captured. But no frogs!

There was a big bowl on his desk filled with
water in which he reared several fishes. He would
occasionally watched the fishes, studying their
movements. Sometimes he would seem to observe
something, and started to draw until the paper was
full of little fishes. He would then stick it on a wall
and sit staring at it till he fell asleep.

My old teacher loved eating crabs, but he kept
crabs as pets too. He often put two crabs on the
floor or in water and watch them walk.

The Seal: "If I had let people down it would be fair they should let
me down."

Abacus (see page 166)

III

An inscription on a painting by Ch'i Pai Shih:

A visitor came requesting me to paint a picture
of "fortune making." I said, "There are so many
ways of making a fortune. What do you want me
to draw?" The visitor said, "Tell me some of the
possibilities." I said, "You want a picture of
Generalissimo Chao?" He said, "No, not quite."
"You want me to draw things like an official seal
and costumes?" He said, "No." I said, "What about
swords, drum-sticks, robes, and so on." He said,
"Sorry, no. Suppose you draw an abacus." I said,
"How wonderful! This is indeed a benevolent
contraption. It aims at making money without
doing any harm!" So I painted an abacus with
great despatch. (page 165)

IV

*From Li K'o Jan's "My teacher and his art":.
(Studies on Ch'i Pai Shih)*

My teacher Pai Shih often wrote the phrase
" 天道酬勤 " meaning "heaven rewards the industrious" for young people who sought his auto-
graph. A year before his death he wrote the three
characters " 精於勤 " for me.

The seal: "stone-addict"

166

From Ch'i Pai Shih by "An Ping" (Ming Pao Monthly, Vol. 48):

The Japanese poet and journalist Mr. Tokio Hashimoto was introduced to Ch'i Pai Shih by Chen Shih Ts eng. In his recollections of Ch'i Pai Shih, there is the following passage: "Ch'i Pai Shih showed me over twenty paintings, each four feet long. When I asked him the price he pointed at a sheet of paper pasted on the wall giving the scale of fees, as follows: 'flowers, 1 *yuan* per foot; flowers with bird or insect, 1.50 *yuan* per foot and landscape, 2 *yuan*. I suggested that the prices were too low, less than half of those of Chen Nien and Wang Meng Pai. He smiled but did not answer, as if to say that there was nothing wrong with low price but high volume of sale. I said that it was ridiculous of a Chinese artist to sell paintings by the foot, like selling cloth. But Ch'i Pai Shih remarked, 'That's all right by me. Just call me a cloth-vendor.' "

Hashimoto mentioned also how in 1924 Ch'i Pai Shih visited him and his bride taking with him a ham for a present. He also gave an account of the friendship between Ch'i Pai Shih and Yang Ling Fu, a woman artist. She had violent arguments with Ch'i Pai Shih over the painting of little chicks. She often said disparaging things about Ch'i Pai Shih. Hashimoto heard later from friends that their difference stemmed from a rather unkind, though probably unintentional, remark made by Ch'i: "Old girl, may be the best thing for you to do is to get married." She never became reconciled with Ch'i Pai Shih after that.

Hashimoto's account went further: "His concubine Pao Chu was always by his side. He was thirty to forty years her senior and she was not good looking at all, besides often suffering from asthma. Ch'i asked me, showing a sheet of paper full of shrimps and crabs, how much I thought each was worth. I hesitated, but ventured to suggest that each should be worth more than eight dollars. He said he had to draw many shrimps and crabs in order to save some money against old age.

He loves peanuts and told me that if I wanted to live long, I should eat five or six raw peanuts, unskinned, three times a day. Having said this, he put some peanuts on my palm. Out of politeness I put them in my mouth but had to eject them after a while. He stared at me and smiled wryly. Once in high summer, I rushed into his studio without bothering to knock and found him taking a nap, his body covered with a piece of white cloth but otherwise quite naked. Pao Chu was sitting beside him keeping him cool with a fan. When he stood up he held the white cloth in his hand and said, "Mr. Hashimoto said I was a cloth-vendor. He has come to buy cloth from me."

At the Sino-Japanese Art Exhibition, one of his paintings was sold at the price of 150 yen. This was a source of encouragement to him. Chen Shih Ts eng was instrumental in introducing him to the Japanese public. Chen died soon after and when I mentioned his name, Ch'i Pai Shih quickly ran outside his studio and wept bitterly."

Mr. Hanai Sato first met Ch'i Pai Shih in 1920. "When people asked for his paintings he would tell his wife to take some out from a chest. When a painting was chosen and he was requested to do an inscription, he would take up a rather worn out brush and effortlessly write a piece of satire or social comment according to the subject painted.

I remembered I paid him at first five dollars for a painting. Afterwards I paid seven, not because he requested it but because I thought that was more appropriate.

He disliked social gatherings. He said that at his age he should not be too active. He sometimes liked to sit in the sun for the sake of health."

"I passively watch you walk"

VI

From Hsu Pei Hung's Art by Chan Fung Hsiang (Ming Pao monthly, November 1971, Volume 6 No. 11)

In 1929, Hsu Pei Hung, President of the Peking Conservatory of Art, became acquainted with Ch'i Pai Shih. It was at the time when Ch'i Pai Shih's style of painting was under attack, but Hsu not only came to his defence but also invited him to teach, having visited him thrice at his home on Borrowed Hill. At first Ch'i demurred, but finally yielded. Two lines in a poem at this time records the episode.

> "How can I refuse him who visited me thrice
>   at my cottage —
> A poor old painter like myself"

Another poem in reply to Hsu reads:

> "In youth I portrayed the hills and streams
> To amuse myself, not to curry the world's
>   favour.
> A thousand tongues defile me for my wayward
>   style —
> Only Hsu, south of the Yangtze, came to my
>   defence.
> He says a strange power emanates from my
>   heart and hand
> Swayed by the spirits — no human work.
> Alas! He was only one against ten thousand —
> The thought fills me with shame and in-
>   dignation"

In a letter to Hsu, Ch'i says:

"It was my parents who gave me birth;
It is you, my friend, who understand me"

The Seal: "The spirits have inspired this, not human skill."

The seal: "I shall study as long as
I can breathe"

MORE SEALS

The seal: "Heaven rewards the industrious"

L to R

"In distress, friendship is put to test."
"Favour received should not be forgotten."

L to R

"Despised by the common herd."
"Only the plum-blossoms know me."

176

L to R

"A person whose conduct is superior is
always disapproved by the crowd."

"Do not talk about others' weaknesses."

L to R

"The superior man is tolerant."
"An empty name is only worth a laugh."

178

L to R

"Three Types of Overplus"
"Poverty is no cause for shame if one is healthy"
"For the people"

L to R

"A old man, why should I behave like a circus monkey"
"I think of home, having left my village long"
"Boiling stone"

180

L to R

"Old man Ping has a son"
"Inkstone farm"
"Old man of Borrowed Hill"

Two sides of a seal

L to R

"Sunset on horseback, flowers beneath the ramparts"
"A thousand autumns"

L to R

"After all, there is nothing like leisure"
"Old but healthy, I do not wish to be an immortal"

SOURCES

參考資料

齊白石詩文篆刻集 陳凡編 香港上海

齊白石作品集 北京人民美術

齊白石研究 上海人民美術

白石詩草

齊白石年譜 胡適編

細說齊白石 薛慧山 大人雜誌

齊白石逸事 安萍 明報月刊

齊白石與黃賓虹 薛慧山 大人雜誌

185

APPENDIX

Pages 189—191: from the *"Mustard Seed Garden."*

Pages 192—5:   specimens of paintings by some artists that have influenced Ch'i Pai Shih — Chu Ta, Hs'u Wei, Shih Tao and Wu Chang Shih.

Pages 196—8:   specimens of paintings by some contemporaries of Chi Pai Shih — Ch'en Shih Tseng, Huang Pin Hung and Hs'u Pei Hung.

Pages from *The Mustardseed Garden Manual of Painting* from which Ch'i Pai Shih learned the elements of drawing.

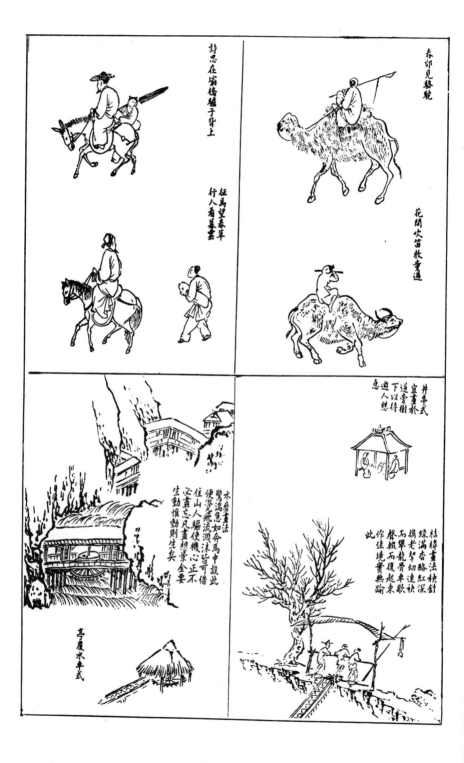

春郊見駱駝

詩思在蹇橋驢子背上

征馬望春草
行人看暮雲

花間吹笛牧童過

井亭式
宜畫於
道旁樹
下以待
遊人憩
息

水磨畫法
驚湍急溜如令馬中設此
便覺飛流濺沫皆可借
住山人驅使機心正不
必盡忘凡畫想景全要
生動惟動景則生矣

桔槔畫法秧針
綠滿杏酪紅深
攜老挈幼連袂
而舉龍骨車而
聲軋軋歌起束
作佳境實無踰
此

高廠水車式

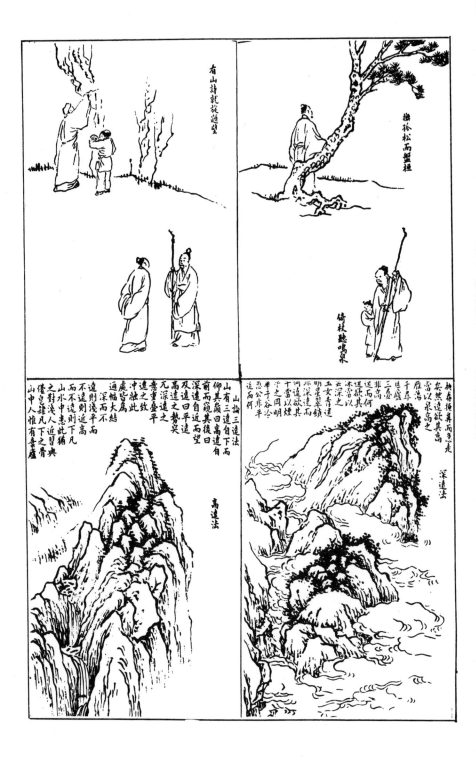

有山排闼就蹉躍

攀孤松而盤桓

倚杖聽鳴泉

山論三遠法
山有三遠自下而
仰其巔曰高遠自
前而窺其後曰深遠
及遠曰平遠
深遠自近而望
高遠之勢突兀
深遠之意重疊
平遠之致沖融
無深遠則
淺而不深
無高遠則
下而不高
通幅大結
遠則淺平而
不遠則近而
山水中惠此
之對淺人近習典
傅皆難凡下之骨
山中人惟有塵廛

高遠法

深遠法

By Hsu Wei

By Chu Ta

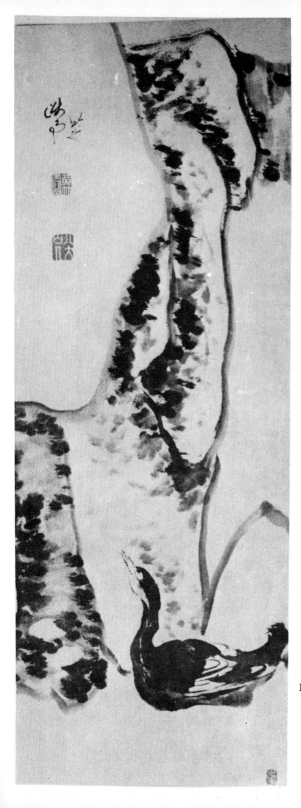

By Chu Ta (Pa Ta Shan Jen)

獨在異鄉為異客 每逢佳節倍思親 遙知兄弟登高處 遍插茱萸少一人

王維九日憶山中兄弟作 余以范寬筆意寫之 清湘濟

By Shih Tao

By Shih Tao

By Wu Chang Shih

By Ch'en Shih Tseng

Huang Pin Hung

By Hsu Pei H

GLOSSARY

GLOSSARY

Ah Chih	阿芝
An Ping	安萍
Chang Chou	常州
Chang Chung Chêng	張中正
Chang Chung Yang	張仲颺
Chang Garden	張園
Ch'ang Hsing Chi	長慶集
Chang Kuang Chi	張筐溪
Chang Li Chi	張立齋
Chang Pô Chên	張柏楨
Ch'ang sha	長沙
Chan Tao-fan	張道藩
Chang Tung	張同
Chang Tz'u Chi	張次溪
Chang Tzu Huan	張紫環
Chao Chih Ch'ien	趙之謙
Chao Hui Shu	趙撝叔
Chen Ch'un Chun	陳春君
Chen Fu Ken	陳茯根
Chen Nien	陳年
Chan Pan Ting	陳半丁
Ch'en San Yüan	陳散原
Ch'en Shih I	陳石遺
Ch'en Shih Ts eng	陳師曾
Ch'en Tso Hsun	陳作壎
Ch'êng Ch'üan Fu	程全父
Ch'i Ch'ang Ling	齊長齡

Chi Huan Hsien Nu	寄幻仙奴
Ch'i Huang	齊璜
Ch'i Pai Shih	齊白石
Ch'i Pe Chang	齊伯常
Chi P'ing	寄萍
Chi P'ing T'ang Chu Jen	寄萍堂主人
Chi Shan	寄禪
Ch'i Shun Chih	齊純芝
Ch'i Ta	齊大
Ch'i Ta Fei Ou	齊大非耦
Chi Yuan	寄園
Chieh Shan Kuan/Borrowed-Hill Chamber	借山館
Chieh Shan T'u Chuan	借山圖卷
Chieh Shan Weng/Borrowed Hill Old Man	借山翁
Chieh Shan Yin Kuan Chu Che	借山吟館主者
Chieh Shan Yin Kuan Shih Ts'ao	借山吟館詩草
Chien Lung	乾隆
Ch'in Chou	欽洲
Chin Sung Ch'en	金松岑
Chin Tung Hsin	金冬心
Ch'ing Ch'êng	青城
Chiu Chiang	九江
Ch'iu Chiang Kuan	秋薑館
Chou	周
Chou Chih Mei	周之美
Chou Yu Yeh	周雨若
Chu Ju	菊如
Chu Po Lu	朱柏廬
Ch'u Shih Ch'i Pai Shih Chih Mu	處士齊白石之墓
Chu Ta	朱耷（八大山人）
Chu Wu Yuan	朱悟園

Chuang Yuan	狀元
Eh Chin Tieh T'ang Yin P'u	二金蝶堂印譜
Fa Yuan Shrine	法源寺
Fan Ts'en Hsiang	樊增祥
Fang Hsü	方旭
Feng Lin Ting	楓林亭
Fu Jê University	輔仁大學
Fu Shih	副室
Han	漢
Heng Mountains	衡山
Heng Yang	衡陽
Ho Li Chih	賀履之
Ho Shao Chi	何紹基
Hsi Chuan	西磚
Hsia Wên Chu	夏文珠
Hsia Wu I	夏午詒
Hsiang T'an	湘潭
Hsiang Tomb	香塚
Hsiao Fang Chün	蕭方駿
Hsiao Hsiang Kai	蕭薌陔
Hsieh Hui Shan	薛慧山
Hsieh P'an	薛蟠
Hsing Tou T'ang/Star Pond	星斗塘
Hsing Tzu Wu/Apricot Valley	杏子塢
Hsü Pei Hung	徐悲鴻
Hsü Po Jao	徐伯郊
Hsü Shen Yu	徐森玉
Hsü Wei	徐渭
Hu Ch'in Yüan	胡沁園
Hu Lêng An	胡冷庵
Hu Li San	胡立三

Hu Lieh Shih	胡廉石
Hu Pao Chu	胡寶珠
Hu T'ung	胡同
Hua Shan	華山
Huang	璜
Huang Hsiao Sung	黃小松
Huang K'o Ch'iang	黃克強（黃興）
Huang Mao Tui Tsu	黃茅堆子
Huang Pin Hung	黃賓虹
Huang Shan Ku	黃山谷
Hunan	湖南
I Shih Fu	易實甫
Kao Yao	高要
Kiangsu	江蘇
Kung Fu	公甫
Kuo Pao Sheng	郭葆生
Kwangsi	廣西
Kwangtung	廣東
Kweilin	桂林
Lan Ting	蘭亭
Lao P'ing	老萍
Li Ch'ing An	黎鯨庵
Li K'o Jan	李可染
Li K'u Shan	李苦禪
Li Sung An	黎松安
Li T'ieh An	黎鐵安
Li Wei Sun	黎薇蓀
Li Yün An	李筠庵
Liang Chih	艮止
Liang Ch'ih	艮遲
Liang Fu	艮黼
Liang Huan	艮歡

206

Liang I	艮巳
Liang Kun	艮琨
Liang Mo	艮末
Liang Nien	艮年
Liang Yüan	艮元
Liao Tung Yin Kuan	遼東吟館
Lin Ch'in Nan	林琴南
Lin Fêng Mien	林風眠
Ling Wên Yuan	凌文淵
Liu Li Ch'ang	琉璃廠
Lo Chen Wu	羅眞吾
Lo Hsing Wu	羅醒吾
Lo Shan Poetry Society	羅山詩社
Lo Tun Nuan	羅惇㬊
Lo Tun Yung	羅惇曧
Lu Shan	廬山
Mei Kung Shrine	梅公祠
Mei Lan Fang	梅蘭芳
Mu Lan	木蘭
O Mei	峨嵋
Pai Shih Hsien Sheng	白石先生
Pai Shih P'u/White Stone Market	白石鋪
Pin	瀕
Pin K'ai Nan	賓愷南
Pin Sheng	瀕生
P'ing	萍
Ping Ling	秉靈
Ping Shêng	秉聲
P'ing Weng	萍翁
Pu Hsin Yu	溥心畬
San Yeh	三爺
Shen Yang	瀋陽

207

Shih Yeh	十爺
Shou Shan Stone	壽山石
Shui Ch'e	水車
Shui Kuang	瑞光
Shun Chih	純芝
Shun Chu	純藻
Shun Ch'üan	純雋
Shun Pei	純培
Sian	西安
Su Lao Chuan	蘇老泉
Su Shih	蘇軾
Sung	宋
Sung Shan	嵩山
T'an Li Sheng	譚荔生
T'an Tsu Ch'üan	譚子荃
T'an Yen K'ai	譚延闓
Tang Shan	碭山
Tao Chi	道濟
Tao Chiai	道階
T'ao jan Ting	陶然亭
Tien hsin	點心
Ting	丁
Ting Hu	鼎湖
Ting Lung Hung	丁龍泓
Ts'ai O	蔡鍔
Ts'eng Chao Chi	曾招吉
Ts'eng Hsi	曾熙
Ts'eng Kuo Fan	曾國藩
Tuan Chi	端溪
T'ung Ch'ih	同治
T'ung Mêng Hui	同盟會
Tzu Ching Hill	紫荊山

Wan An Cemetery	萬安公墓
Wan Li Lou	萬里樓
Wang Chi Lin	汪吉麟
Wang Chung Yen	王仲言
Wang Hsiang Ch'i	王湘綺（閣運）
Wang Meng Pai	王夢白
Wang Sung Nien	汪頌年
Wang Yün	王雲
Wei Ch'ing	渭清
Wen Chi	文姬
Wo Lan I Tz'u	握蘭簃詞
Wu Ch'ang Shih	吳昌碩
Wu Pê Chiang	吳兆江
Wu Shih Chai	烏石寨
Yang Ling Fu	楊令茀
Yang Pu Chih	楊補之
Yang Shuo	陽朔
Yang Yün Shih	楊雲史
Yao Hua	姚華
Yao Wu Shuang	姚無雙
Yeh Chien Yu	葉淺予
Yen Tun Ling	煙墩嶺
Ying Wu Tomb	鸚鵡塚
Yung Lo	永樂